An Outdoor Family Guide to

THE SOUTHWEST'S
FOUR CORNERS

An Outdoor Family Guide to

THE SOUTHWEST'S FOUR CORNERS

Tom and Gayen Wharton

THE
MOUNTAINEERS

To our children, Emma, Jacob, Rawl, and Bryer, who thank
us today for their strong hearts, lungs, and legs because we "hiked
them into the ground!" when they were young.

 Published by
The Mountaineers
1001 SW Klickitat Way, Suite 201
Seattle, WA 98134

9 8 7 6 5
5 4 3 2 1

Published simultaneously in Canada by Douglas & McIntyre, Ltd., 1615
Venables Street, Vancouver, B.C. V5L 2H1

Published simultaneously in Great Britain by Cordee,
3a DeMontfort Street, Leicester, England, LE1 7HD

Manufactured in the United States of America

Edited by Heath Lynn Silberfeld
Maps by Mark Knudsen
Photographs by Tom Wharton and Reb Staks (Bandelier National Monument)
Cover design by The Mountaineers Books
Book design and typography by The Mountaineers Books
Book layout by WordGraphics

Cover photograph: *Shiprock, New Mexico* © David Muench/Tony Stone Images.
   Inset: *Winter scene at Zion National Park, Utah*
Frontispiece: *A breathtaking view of the Grand Canyon*

Library of Congress Cataloging-in-Publication Data

Wharton, Tom, 1950–
    An outdoor family guide to the Southwest's Four Corners / Tom and Gayen
Wharton.
       p.   cm.
    Includes index.
    ISBN 0-89886-407-0
    1. Outdoor recreation—Southwest, New—Guidebooks.   2. Family
recreation—Southwest, New—Guidebooks.   3. Southwest, New—
Guidebooks.   I. Wharton, Gayen, 1950–   .   II. Title.
GV191.42.S68W43   1995
917.904'33—dc20   95–23138
                                                                        CIP

Contents

1. Wupatki National Monument
2. Sunset Crater Volcano National Monument
3. Walnut Canyon National Monument
4. Montezuma Castle National Monument
5. Grand Canyon National Park
6. Glen Canyon National Recreation Area
7. Rainbow Bridge National Monument
8. Pipe Spring National Monument
9. Petrified Forest National Park
10. Canyon de Chelly National Monument

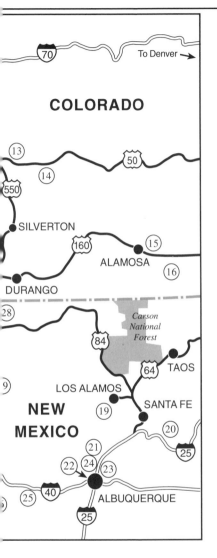

11. Rabbit Valley
12. Colorado National Monument
13. Black Canyon of the Gunnison National Monument
14. Curecanti National Recreation Area

15. Great Sand Dunes National Monument
16. Alamosa National Wildlife Refuge
17. Mesa Verde National Park
18. Anasazi Heritage Center
19. Bandelier National Monument
20. Pecos National Monument
21. Coronado State Park
22. Rio Grande Nature Center
23. Sandia Mountain
24. Petroglyph National Monument
25. Acoma Pueblo
26. El Malpais National Monument
27. El Morro National Monument
28. Aztec Ruins National Monument
29. Chaco Canyon National Historical Park
30. Zion National Park
31. Dixie Red Cliffs
32. Snow Canyon State Park
33. Coral Pink Sand Dunes State Park
34. Cedar Breaks National Monument
35. Fremont Indian State Park
36. Capitol Reef National Park
37. Goblin Valley State Park
38. Natural Bridges National Monument
39. Bryce Canyon National Park
40. Kodachrome Basin State Park
41. Escalante State Park
42. Anasazi Indian Village State Park
43. Canyonlands National Park
44. Arches National Park
45. Hovenweep National Monument
46. Edge of the Cedars State Park
47. Dinosaur National Monument

Introduction

Alone one morning, a family walked through a narrow Southwestern canyon, looking up in awe at its convoluted red sandstone walls. The distinctive whistles of canyon wrens broke the morning silence. Walking past cottonwood trees growing along the banks of a tiny river, the family examined the footprints of deer, raccoons, coyotes, mice, and squirrels that had ventured into the canyon the night before. There was time to skip stones in the river, sit alone in an alcove, or study clouds moving across a blue sky.

Searching for signs of ancient Anasazi Indians, the parents told their children to examine the canyon walls for a ruin or rock writing. Was that a small arch on the canyon horizon? What kind of plant is that? Was that a hawk or an eagle?

As a teenager trotted ahead of the group so she could take time to write observations in her nature journal, the father told the youngest family member a story. Mom took time to photograph a blooming prickly pear cactus, a buffaloberry plant, and a juniper tree.

The family spent much of the day alone in this remote canyon feeling very much alive and learning many self-taught lessons. Parents and children enjoyed what could best be described as a natural high, all the while taking great care not to damage this special place.

The Four Corners area of Utah, Arizona, New Mexico, and Colorado—the colorful Colorado Plateau—offers many such adventures for families. Take a wild raft ride down the Colorado River or enjoy a quiet canoe trip through a red rock wilderness. Board an old steam train and ride it through the rugged Rocky Mountains. Ride a mule down a narrow Grand Canyon trail or ride like a cowboy on the back of a horse in a land where Butch Cassidy once roamed. Finesse a mountain bike across a petrified red rock sand dune.

Spend an evening in a quiet campground sleeping on fine red sand or the black cinders of an ancient volcano. Take time to simply enjoy a campfire and each other's company. Learn the lessons of the past by reading, watching, and listening. Use a telescope to explore the crystal clear Southwestern skies.

Mostly, take time to explore the incredible, unmatched scenery of the Colorado Plateau on foot. Your family won't have to hike far, sometimes less than 0.5 mile, to wander under arches and natural bridges or discover canyons so narrow mom and dad may have trouble squeezing through. Hikes lead into twisting canyons, to tops of mountains, to Indian ruins, and through different types of forests.

The purpose of this book is to help families explore the Southwest together in a variety of different environments. Few areas in the world contain as many national parks and monuments, national forests, state parks, and public lands concentrated in a single area. Diverse cultures—such as Hopi, Navajo, and Hispanic—combine with that of the traditional Western cowboy. Add modern towns offering many amenities and attractions to this mix, and families have the basis for a most memorable outdoor vacation.

The greatest task most will face is deciding which places to visit.

Each member of a family stands in a different state at the Four Corners Monument.

Using This Book

This is a guidebook for active, outdoor-oriented families. Since camping and hiking are the easiest and least expensive way to see the Southwest, each chapter describes a number of alternatives that allow enjoyment of both activities. The book is also written with information on the availability of lodging inside parks or at nearby towns.

Because young legs often cannot handle long treks with great elevation gains, the vast majority of the hikes in this book are under 5 miles. Many are self-guided nature trails that give children a chance to learn not only about the Southwest's unique environment but also make them want to finish a trail as they follow detailed trail guides.

Descriptions of hikes in this book are brief. The idea is to give parents a feel for the difficulty of the walk and what their family will see. More detailed children's hiking guides, as well as books with longer hikes and backpacking adventures in this area, are available from The Mountaineers.

Introductory material is designed to give parents an idea of things to do besides hiking. Most National Park Service properties in the Four Corners region, for example, host Junior Ranger programs. Cities feature museums and amusements geared to families. Commercial activities like steam-train rides, rafting trips, horseback and mule rides, mountain bike adventures, skiing, snowshoeing, and four-wheel-driving deliver variety to families. Where appropriate, camping possibilities are listed.

This book concentrates on the red rock canyon country and high mountain alpine zones of the Four Corners region of southern Utah, northern Arizona, southeastern Colorado, and northeastern New Mexico. Though emphasis has been placed on visiting national parks and monuments, suggestions in each chapter point to less visited state parks, national forests, and Bureau of Land Management public lands.

Part of the fun of a family vacation involves allowing children to participate in the planning process. In the appendix at the back of the book, look for addresses where children can write for free information and reading material.

Take time to allow children to play in the sand.

When to Go

With the exception of times when kids have yet to reach school age or they attend school year-round, most families must travel in the summer when school is out of session. In the case of many Southwest destinations, that is somewhat unfortunate because summer is the hottest, most crowded, and most expensive time of year to visit the Southwest's parks and monuments.

Does that mean a family should avoid the Southwest in the summer? Definitely not. There are more interpretive activities, evening programs, and special events that enhance a family vacation to the parks and monuments during the busier tourist season. In many cases, nearby national forest lands in the high country provide places to hike and camp where summer's heat can be avoided.

What it does mean is that families should make summer camping reservations where possible. In parks with no reservation systems, campers should arrive early. If planning to stay in a lodge or motel, families should make reservations ahead of time. The same holds true for four-wheel-drive, mountain biking, and river rafting tours.

For families who want to take a short vacation in the off-season, the proximity of outdoor activities to urban areas in the Four Corners region makes the area particularly attractive. A three-day weekend holiday in the spring, fall, or winter can include numerous recreation possibilities. Seeing this country covered with snow or enjoying the wildflowers of spring or the fall colors in comparative solitude furnishes a different perspective from that of summer. Hotel and lodging rates tend to be much less expensive. In the dead of winter, many of the lower-elevation park trails can be enjoyed under cooler circumstances and often free of people. Downhill and cross-country skiing are available throughout the Four Corners region. Seeing red rock country like Bryce Canyon National Park covered with snow on a bright, blue day is a scene most families savor. When planning, though, keep in mind that some popular areas such as the North Rim of the Grand Canyon and Cedar Breaks National Monument close to automobile traffic due to snow.

When taking a Southwest summer vacation, realize that temperatures vary wildly, even in the same general area. At the Grand Canyon, for example, the temperature can often be 30 degrees warmer at the bottom than near the tourist facilities on the rims. National forests only 10 or 15 miles away from the red rock deserts can be cool in summer. Still, keep in mind that many of the desert areas described in this book can and do reach temperatures close to 100 on many June, July, and August afternoons. Plan hikes with your children in the early morning and late evening hours. In the middle of the day, visit museums, see a movie at a nearby town, enjoy a swim, take a nap, or head to higher alpine country, which is often nearby. Temperatures tend to be mildest in the spring and fall.

No matter when you travel in the Southwest, though, come prepared for just about any type of weather condition. It can be cool and rainy in July, and it can be warm and dry in December, depending on the year. An old joke about the Southwest is that if you do not like the weather wait a minute and things will change. That's not far from the truth.

Advantages of Family Camping

At a time when money problems prevent some families from taking vacations, camping offers an inexpensive alternative to staying in motels and eating in restaurants. Camping fees at many public campgrounds—especially in national forests and Bureau of Land Management facilities—often run less than $10 a night. At national park facilities, fees are seldom higher than $10. Add the savings of being able to fix less expensive meals over a gas stove, and an outdoor vacation suddenly becomes more affordable.

Most of the national parks, monuments, and U.S. Forest Service and state parks listed in this book offer camping. A few of the larger camping facilities—like those at the Grand Canyon and Mesa Verde—have showers. So do many of the state parks.

In addition, good private campgrounds are available in gateway communities near major attractions. Though usually costing slightly more, in private campgrounds families often find amenities like swimming pools, miniature golf courses, and arcades that children enjoy after a long day of hiking. Private campgrounds can also be found at the edges of all the cities listed in this book and can be less expensive alternatives to staying in a motel. Besides, when given the choice of staying in a small motel room or having the great outdoors to enjoy, most children prefer the freedom camping gives them. The different things kids find to do in a campground amaze most parents.

That brings up a word of caution. Though campgrounds are outdoors, children cannot be allowed to run totally wild. They should avoid screaming and shouting, especially after sundown, in deference to other campers. Also, while many fun activities can be enjoyed, parents must watch that their children aren't destroying the land by cutting green trees, playing in wet meadows, or digging trenches around tents.

Making a List

Before going on a family vacation—especially one that involves outdoor activities and camping—it is a good idea to make up a list of things to pack. There is nothing more frustrating than being in a remote campground and discovering that an essential item, like a mantel for a gas lantern or a sleeping bag, has accidentally been left behind.

Some families go so far as to put a list of needed items for an outdoor vacation on their home computers. Before every trip the list is printed out, and a family member is assigned to check off each item as it is packed into a motor vehicle.

Here is one such list, including the Ten Essentials you should carry on any hike or backpacking trip:

✔ Extra clothing	✔ First-aid kit	
✔ Extra food	✔ Matches in a waterproof container	
✔ Sunglasses	✔ Flashlight	
✔ Knife	✔ Map	
✔ Fire starter	✔ Compass	

Food Items

☐ Milk	☐ Bread	☐ Butter
☐ Lemon	☐ Cooking oil	☐ Salt
☐ Pepper	☐ Condiments	☐ Sandwich Supplies
☐ Breakfasts	☐ Lunches	☐ Dinners
☐ Snacks		

Personal Items

☐ Suitcases	☐ Coats	☐ Sweatshirts
☐ Socks	☐ Hats	☐ Swimsuits
☐ Underwear	☐ Pants	☐ Shirts
☐ Boots	☐ Sandals	☐ Shoes
☐ Lifejackets	☐ Travel kit	☐ Suntan oil
☐ Sunblock	☐ Towels	☐ Water bottles
☐ Wind pants	☐ Rain clothing	☐ Gloves

Camp Kitchen Supplies

☐ Silverware	☐ Knives	☐ Scouring pad
☐ Dish soap	☐ Hand soap	☐ Dish towels
☐ Water jug	☐ Pans	☐ Can opener
☐ Paper towels	☐ Tablecloth	☐ Sponge
☐ Matches	☐ Dishes	☐ Foil
☐ Garbage bags		

Camping Basics

☐ Tent	☐ Tent poles	☐ Sleeping Bags
☐ Blankets	☐ Lantern	☐ Mantels
☐ Hammer	☐ Toolbox	☐ Stove
☐ Fuel	☐ Flashlight	☐ Daypack
☐ Backpack	☐ Charcoal	☐ Lighter
☐ Cooler	☐ Lounge chairs	☐ Air mattresses

Miscellaneous

☐ Camera	☐ Car games	☐ First-aid kit
☐ Film	☐ Compass	☐ Binoculars
☐ Whistle		

Taking Care of the Land

The deserts and mountains of the Four Corners region rank among the most environmentally sensitive found anywhere in the world. Scars from the abuses of off-highway-vehicle owners, irresponsible campers, vandals, and litterbugs can last for generations. Part of a parent's duty in educating a child is teaching a good land ethic. This is best done by adults who set an example themselves.

That might mean taking along an extra empty sack and picking up litter left along the trail by sloppy hikers. It might involve spending some time cleaning up a campground before leaving it. It could mean reading over park regulations before entering a new area or discussing local laws at the visitor center before heading into the backcountry.

Kids often become the land's biggest advocate. When they know the law and the reason for it, children become offended when other visitors take shortcuts on trails, feed wild animals, steal valuable archaeological artifacts from public lands, or leave campfires burning.

Take time to explain the reasons for special regulations on public land. More importantly, set a good example for your children by learning and practicing "Leave No Trace" camping techniques and "Tread Lightly" mountain bicycle and off-highway-vehicle concepts.

The following are suggestions for taking care of the outdoors made by public land management organizations like the Bureau of Land Management, U.S. Forest Service, National Park Service, Take Pride in Utah, KUED-Channel 7 in Salt Lake City, state parks offices, The Mountaineers, and a variety of other environmental groups:

PROTECTING CULTURAL RESOURCES

For many young and old visitors to the Southwest, visiting an archaeological site can be a new adventure. However, such visits can involve a land ethic completely new to visitors.

Children tend to be collectors, but the taking of rocks from any national park and monument is prohibited. It is always best to leave flowers, rocks, and other natural features undisturbed, even if regulations do not specify just that. The pocketing of bits of ancient pottery, arrowheads, or stones found around any archaeological site on public or private land is also strictly prohibited. These sites are protected by the Antiquities Protection Act of 1906 and the Archaeological Resources Protection Act of 1979. The latter calls for stiff penalties plus a reward for information leading to a conviction. Taking things from an archaeological site is, simply put, stealing from the past. A small, seemingly insignificant piece of evidence removed from an archaeological site might hinder a professional scientist from making important future discoveries. In addition, these sites are considered sacred by Native Americans who regard such acts as a sign of great disrespect. Also, think of the thrill of discovering an ancient artifact in an outdoor setting. If every family took just one piece away, experiences like that would be impossible for future hikers to enjoy.

The National Outdoor Leadership School and the Bureau of Land Management have prepared a set of minimum-impact guidelines offering suggestions on visiting and enjoying archaeological sites of the ancient people who once lived in the Four Corners region. The following information is based upon three pamphlets— BLM/Utah Minimum Impact Guide (Hiking and Backpacking), BLM/Utah Minimum Impact Guide (Cultural Resources), and the National Outdoor Leadership School's "The Minimum-Impact Approach to Desert & Canyon Wildlands":

1. Keep in mind that not entering a site but viewing it from a distance will reduce the impact a site receives. People may say, "It's just a couple of us and it's just one time," but there may be thousands of people saying the same thing.
2. Stop, look, and think before entering a cultural site. Locate the midden area (the trash pile) so you can avoid walking on it. Middens contain important archaeological artifacts and information. Walking over these fragile areas can cause damage.
3. If a trail has been built across a site, stay on it. Foot traffic, especially on a midden, causes erosion that may undermine the walls of structures above.
4. When you see potsherds and other artifacts, leave them.
5. Do not camp in or near ruins. Not only is this practice illegal, but it can damage fragile ruins. The less use a ruin site gets, the longer it will stay preserved.

6. Moving rocks and tree branches to climb to high places destroys site integrity. Avoid touching plaster walls.
7. Enjoy rock art by viewing, sketching, and photographing it. Never chalk, trace, or otherwise touch rock art. Any direct contact can cause these ancient figures to disintegrate.
8. Creating modern rock art is known as vandalism and is punishable by law.
9. Never build fires in alcoves, even alcoves that do not seem to contain archaeological remains. Sites may not be obvious.
10. Climbing on roofs and walls can destroy in a moment that which has lasted for hundreds of years.
11. Cultural sites are places of ancestral importance to Native Americans and should be treated with respect.

MINIMUM IMPACT DESERT CAMPING

Though minimum impact or "Leave No Trace" camping will work in any kind of environment, it is especially important to practice some basic camping techniques in the desert. Life in this arid land depends on complex associations of water and soil.

This is especially true when traveling in places where cryptobiotic soil can be found. This complicated soil, which resembles dark castles, plays an important role in building soil for desert plants. Whenever possible, avoid this black, crusty substance. Walk on established trails and, if there is no other way to avoid it, follow in one another's footsteps.

Following is a list of camping suggestions offered by the Bureau of Land Management, the National Outdoor Leadership School in Lander, Wyoming, and The Mountaineers in Seattle. In general, these "Leave No Trace" programs are also endorsed by the National Park Service and the U.S. Forest Service:

1. Concentrate activities on established trails and campsites. When possible, stay on hard "slickrock" that is devoid of vegetation.
2. The smaller the group, the better. Many land management agencies limit backpacking groups to 12 or under.
3. Slickrock, dry washes, and open ground free of cryptobiotic crust make the best campsites.
4. When possible, choose a campsite that shows obvious signs of use.

5. Protecting water sources in the desert can mean life or death to human, animal, and insect populations. That's because water can be scarce in this area. Camp at least 200 feet from water sources if possible and avoid using water sources after dark. Conserve desert water and use small springs for drinking only. Avoid polluting water sources. Do not wash directly in potholes. Washing should be done at least 200 feet from running water and away from potholes. Wash water should be emptied over sand.

6. Avoid fires if at all possible, and build them only in existing fire rings and only where safe and legally permitted. Gas campstoves work much better and do less damage to the environment. Wood is scarce in the desert. If you must have a fire, make a small one and use a fire pan or blanket to prevent blackening of the soil or rocks. Use only dead or down wood. Do not build fires in alcoves. Leave no evidence of a fire.

7. Use backcountry toilets when available. Because desert soils have few microorganisms to help break down human feces, land managers say extra care must be taken to dispose of human waste properly. They recommend choosing two different types of sites. One can be a place with maximum exposure to direct sunlight. The other can be a place near organic matter such as bushes or trees. Dig shallow holes, no more than four to six inches deep and at least 200 feet from all water sources. Carry out all toilet paper. A good method is to pack fresh toilet paper and an empty locking-type plastic baggie inside a plastic baggie. Use one baggie for "used" toilet paper, the other for "fresh paper."

Safety Tips

Parents must stress to children that, while the outdoors can offer all sorts of safe and fun adventures, careless horseplay and ignoring safety rules can lead to dangerous and deadly situations.

Take hiking, for example. Some of the easiest treks in the Southwest often expose families to hot sun, steep overlooks, and potential confrontations with snakes, scorpions, and biting insects. This means parents must educate their children about potential dangers before going out and, especially where young children are concerned, watch them closely at all times.

Some safety considerations involve simple common sense. Always carry enough water. Take a basic survival kit that includes a Swiss Army Knife (one with tweezers to pull out cactus needles), matches in waterproof container, flashlight, a whistle (to aid in locating help), compass, and rain gear. The Mountaineers has published a guide called The Ten Essentials for Travel in the Outdoors, with details on these basics (also see list of "Ten Essentials" above). A good hat to shade face and head from the sun is a must. On hot summer days, sunblock can prevent painful—if not dangerous—sunburning. Having insect repellent, especially when near wetlands or in high alpine wilderness areas near lakes, is another must. When near water sources, hikers also might consider packing a light water filter in case an emergency arises.

First-aid kits vary. When taking short hikes, a simple, commercially produced kit that includes adhesive bandages, children's bandages, patch bandages, alcohol cleansing pads, iodine prep pads, antiseptic, towelettes, triple-antibacterial cream, and sting relief pads works well. It weighs only a few ounces and takes little space. A more heavy-duty kit containing gauze, elastic bandages, ammonia inhalants, aspirin tablets, scissors, insect repellents, and blankets and splints can be stored in your motor vehicle or at camp.

Having a first-aid kit is one thing. Knowing how to use it is another. Taking a basic course in first aid and CPR (cardio-pulmonary resuscitation) through school, scouts, or work is a good idea. Carrying reminders on how to use this knowledge can be helpful, too, especially in a crisis situation. Brunton USA of Riverton, Wyoming, for example, sells a Life Card system that easily fits in a wallet. It includes basic survival equipment like a compass and magnifying glass as well as instructions for basic first-aid techniques for all types of situations. A number of publishers issue pocket guides about first aid that take up little room in a pack. The Southwestern Region of the U.S. Forest Service publishes a free "On Your Own in Southwestern Mountains" booklet (write to USDA Forest Service, Public Affairs Office, 517 Gold Avenue SW, Albuquerque, NM 87102 or visit any district ranger office). It includes safety information as well as tips for recognition, symptoms, and treatment of heat stress and hypothermia. It contains information on emergency preparedness, how to send emergency signals to search-and-rescue groups, and how to acclimatize to higher altitudes.

Watching the weather can be extremely important. This is true especially in the summer when sudden thunderstorms can create flash flood situations or threaten hikers exposed in barren desert areas.

Parents need to stress to their children the importance of staying on the trail and staying together. In the case of toddlers under three, using a harness that allows children to walk but restrains them from dangerous situations works well. Parents should tell their children to stay within sight of one another at all times. It might be necessary to station one adult at the front of a group and another at the rear to make certain that fast hikers do not get too far ahead and stragglers do not get left behind. Parents should also stress the importance of not throwing rocks on a trail. Many Southwestern hikes involve walking up switchbacks. Tossing rocks can injure hikers on lower portions of trails, as well as add to erosion problems and trail debris.

Another important safety consideration involves staying away from wildlife. Feeding wildlife often leads to bites and disease and can hasten the destruction of wild creatures. Larger predatory animals like bears, raccoons, and mountain lions can inhabit some of the outdoor areas in the Four Corners region. Locking up all food or hanging it out of the reach of animals (4 feet from tree trunk and 8 feet off the ground) and keeping a clean camp can help keep a family safe.

The Hantavirus disease has proved to be a problem in the Southwest in recent years. To prevent this disease, avoid contact with pack rat trash heaps, middens, rodent feces, or nests, and with small mammals.

Traveling Tips

The Four Corners area of Utah, Colorado, New Mexico, and Arizona covered in this book includes a large area. In many cases, parks or family fun activities are miles away. Knowing a few travel techniques can help make for a more enjoyable journey.

Toddlers under the age of four can do a considerable amount of walking. While carrying a child allows adults to cover more ground, youngsters soon get bored. Kids who hike get a chance to feel and explore a new world. What's more, sleeping in a strange environment like a tent, motorhome, trailer, or motel room can be disconcerting to younger children, but a child who has spent a day walking and exploring will be tired and will get to sleep easier.

A good driving idea is to leave early in the morning, allowing children to quietly sleep in the back of the vehicle for three or four hours. Then, when children are awake, it is important to take many stops along the way. Look for parks with restrooms and playgrounds. Public swimming pools, which are found in most small towns, can provide a wonderful break in the middle of the day.

Most automobiles—even rentals—are equipped with tape players. Check out a number of story tapes from a local library and play them to keep children's interest. Car games work well. Try putting together a "surprise goody bag" where children get to pull one "surprise" out each day. Surprises can include comic books, games, maps, or other goodies. Parents can read novels or stories along the way to keep their children from bickering in the back seat.

Travel as an Educational Tool

The world is the best classroom. Children who have firsthand experience of subjects can more easily apply them to classroom situations. Educational opportunities in the Southwest are as varied as the region.

One popular method for teaching geography involves visiting the Four Corners Monument. This is the only place in the United States where a person can stand in one place and be in four states—Utah, Colorado, New Mexico and Arizona—at the same time. A visit to this spot, where children create many ways to be in four states at the same time, is fun.

Another vacation skill that can help later in school is the art of map reading, which children can learn at an early age. Use maps along the way to show them where they are and where they are going, eliminating the common "Are we there yet?" questions.

Nature guides available in many places get kids oriented to recognizing landmarks. As children mature, they can be taught to use landmarks as a means to keep from getting lost.

The Southwest has many distinct ecosystems that can be compared in different places. Children can use indicator species of plants to identify which ecosystem they are exploring. The adaptations of each ecosystem can be explored using interpretive materials available in the parks. Children can find the thick waxy leaves of buffaloberry or prickly pear cactus preserving water in the desert areas and the tall cottonwoods, with their huge canopies, taking advantage of underground water along river washes. There are forests of ponderosa pine and Douglas fir where water is more prevalent and forests of pinyon and juniper where it is not.

Children can also listen and look for the animals, large and small, that inhabit these ecosystems. For a mental stretch and some fun, have children identify plants or animals that most resemble them either in physical or emotional characteristics.

During the day is a great time to slow down and have children write or draw in journals. Record both accurate representations of what is seen and impressions and emotions that have been gathered, or have children take their own photos to be arranged in albums and identified. These memories will be as priceless as any souvenir.

The cultural fabric of the Southwest is rich and easily identified by children. Look first for signs of a "foreign" language: Spanish. Point out that most of the streets, cities, and states may have been named while the area was indeed a foreign country: Mexico. A simple Spanish-English dictionary can be the springboard to foreign language study. Have children find things that are different from home: food, architecture, and physical characteristics of the inhabitants. Model acceptance of these differences. Attend a cultural event such as a pueblo feast day or Spanish market to savor the sights, sounds, smells, and tastes of this culture.

Nowhere else in the United States is there a better chance to learn from Native Americans. From ancient Anasazi to modern Hopi and Navajo, the arts and crafts, architecture, foods, and ways of life of native cultures are abundant. It is also easy for children to strike up a conversation with a Native American on the street, in the shops, or parks and to compare history and lifestyles.

It is especially while hiking, however, that visitors can sense what the cultures of the Southwest are all about. It is the stark beauty, the solitariness of the desert, that centuries of people have enjoyed. It is the prudent use of water that ensures survival. It is centuries of tradition that form a character unique in the world.

A NOTE ABOUT SAFETY

Safety is an important concern in all outdoor activities. No guidebook can alert you to every hazard or anticipate the limitations of every reader. Therefore, the descriptions of roads, trails, routes, and natural features in this book are not representations that a particular place or excursion will be safe for your party. When you follow any of the routes described in this book, you assume responsibility for your own safety. Under normal conditions, such excursions require the usual attention to traffic, road and trail conditions, weather, terrain, the capabilities of your party, and other factors. Keeping informed on current conditions and exercising common sense are the keys to a safe, enjoyable outing.

The Mountaineers

Forest hikes can be found next to desert scenery.

Arizona

Northern Arizona is a land of painted deserts, lonely Navajo towns, and long stretches of uninhabited highways marked by scenic vistas. But, to much of the world, only three words apply to this colorful area: The Grand Canyon.

This deep canyon gorge, cut over millions of years by the rushing waters of the Colorado River, defines northern Arizona. For thousands of families throughout the world, it is a destination not to be missed. With good reason. The opportunity to take a mule ride down a winding trail, raft the challenging whitewater of the Colorado River, or simply stand at an overlook near a historical lodge watching the sunset over the canyon draws families from all over the world to the Grand Canyon.

However, thousands of visitors make the mistake of seeing only the Grand Canyon, ignoring the other pleasures of northern Arizona. This is a land of ancient Indian ruins marked by the eruptions of now silent volcanoes. It is a place of high alpine forests where downhill skiers and snowmobilers play. Families gather in Oak Creek Canyon south of Flagstaff to splash in waterfalls. They tour art galleries and dine at upscale restaurants in Sedona. They discover the magic of visiting the Navajo Reservation and seeing places like Canyon de Chelly National Monument. Families walk next to giant petrified trees in a desolate land where dinosaurs once roamed. They hike through lava tube caves using the light of lanterns and flashlights or backpack into pristine wilderness areas. They boat across the waters of Lake Powell or marvel at wondrous feats of engineering while touring Glen Canyon Dam.

Northern Arizona is a place of colors, contrasts, and beauty with more than enough activities to keep children entranced for weeks.

Flagstaff

This city of over 45,000 residents serves as a hub for many northern Arizona family vacations. Located 78 miles from the south rim of the Grand Canyon, Flagstaff is surrounded by national forests and monuments. Many families choose to make the city headquarters for a trip to northern Arizona, either camping in a Coconino National Forest facility or a private campground or staying in one of numerous Flagstaff motels.

Within a few hours, those staying in Flagstaff can visit Sunset Crater Volcano, Wupatki, Tuzigoot, Montezuma Castle, or Walnut Canyon national monuments. They can enjoy a day hike or a dip in the stream at popular Oak Creek Canyon. They can visit Sedona, ski at the Arizona Snowbowl, or enjoy a mountain bike ride in the Coconino National Forest, which surrounds the town.

This is not to say there are not family activities to enjoy right in the city. An extensive urban trail system makes bicycling or walking through town or in the nearby forest easy. Because Flagstaff is the home of Northern Arizona University, it serves as the

Hiking in Wupatki National Monument

hub for a number of good educational activities. These include the Museum of Arizona with displays of artwork and Anasazi artifacts, the modern 200-acre Arboretum at Flagstaff, and the Lowell Observatory, the place where the planet Pluto was first discovered in 1930.

Wupatki National Monument

This 56-square-mile national monument, established in 1924, is located west of the Little Colorado River in northern Arizona's Painted Desert. A 35-mile paved loop road starts and ends off US 89 north of Flagstaff and connects Wupatki with Sunset Crater Volcano National Monument. Neither offers camping, but there is a U.S. Forest Service facility near the entrance to Sunset Crater Volcano.

For information on camping, write to Coconino National Forest, Peaks Ranger Station, 5010 N. Highway 89, Flagstaff, AZ

86004. The visitor center, site of the main ruins and a small museum, is open from 8:00 A.M. to 6:00 P.M. Memorial Day through Labor Day. There are four short developed trails inside the monument, none longer than 0.5 mile. Longer ranger-guided hikes are sometimes available on the weekends during the summer. The elevation ranges between 4,500 and 5,500 feet. By hiking less than 0.5 mile on a Wupatki National Monument trail, a family can stroll back 800 years into history. Wind still blasts out of tiny cracks in the earth, and a culture that left no written words has built amazingly sophisticated communities in this harsh desert climate.

The longest of the four major hikes in this national monument north of Flagstaff is only 0.5 mile long, but parents who think that the number of miles walked equates to more of a quality experience might be fooled. These four hikes challenge the intellect of young and old. Start at the visitor center. Wander through the small museum and learn about the culture of the peoples who occupied this site from A.D. 1120 to A.D. 1210. Modern-day Hopi call these people the Hisatsinom (people of long ago). Archaeologists refer to them as the Sinagua, Anasazi, and Cohonino. In the small museum, visitors are invited to touch replicas of pots and bones found near the site. They can examine pottery sherds. These touchstones provide the foundation for the hike that follows.

Wupatki National Monument is home to an example of what, at first glance, appears to be a simple roadside attraction that can be viewed in 15 minutes on the way to something better. It is much more. Those who take the time to sit, watch, and contemplate while hiking its short trails will likely be surprised at the intellectual family discussions that follow.

Wupatki Ruin Trail

0.5 mile, loop, year-round

When walking the 0.5-mile trail to the Wupatki Ruin that starts and ends at the visitor center, pick up a children's activity book from the ranger. Young hikers who complete the workbook receive a Junior Ranger badge at the end of the hike. The real reward, though, will come when a child begins completing the workbook.

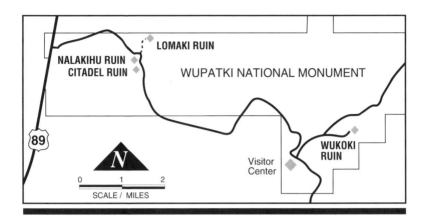

Park rangers designed the small guide to encourage young naturalists to observe the world around them. This is a place of clear blue skies, red sandstone laced with black cinders from nearby volcanoes, and mysterious ruins of homes built long ago. The book asks Junior Rangers to write a poem, name a plant, watch a lizard, reveal their feelings, and, most important, preserve the ruins.

Negotiating a narrow trail at Wupatki National Monument

The best part of this hike comes at the midway point of the trail, about 0.25 mile from the visitor center. Hikers stand over a blowhole where they feel a blast of cool air coming from the earth. Expect children to ask questions like "Where does the wind come from?" "Why is it cool?" "Does it always blow?" "Did ancient people feel this hole connected them to the spirit world?" Most adults won't know the answers. Those who do likely picked up the free explanatory brochure from the ranger at the front desk of the visitor center. Let children wonder and speculate before giving them the answers.

A number of these blowholes, some of which emit or take in volumes of air at up to 35 miles per hour, can be found throughout the monument. The one at the edge of the Wupatki Ruin has been sterilized a bit by the National Park Service, largely for safety purposes. It is marked by a platform of rocks. A heavy mesh screen covers the hole. Hikers stand above the hole and, when conditions are right, a blast of cold air from the earth hits them in the face. In reality, there is nothing mysterious about blowholes. These cracks in the earth respond to barometric air pressure. If that pressure is less on the outside, air blows out. If it is greater, air is sucked into the earth. Surprisingly, no evidence exists that native people ever regarded the air currents as earth spirits or gods, but since no written records from these people exist, the concept is not totally implausible.

Wupatki's best-known feature is its ancient ball court. This oval-shaped masonry ruin is similar to those of southern Arizona and northern New Mexico. Archaeologists are still unsure of its use.

From the ball court, hikers walk along the other side of the ruin back to the visitor center. At this point, many visitors might be tempted to skip the three other major trails at the monument and rush to nearby Sunset Crater Volcano or the Grand Canyon. Unfortunately, those who do will miss the best part of the park.

Wukoki, Citadel, Nalakihu, Lomaki Ruins

*Wukoki, Citadel, and Nalakihu lie next to roadside pullouts,
and Lomaki is 0.5 mile off the main loop road,
one-way, year-round*

Because of heavy visitation to Wupatki Ruin, restrictions are quite tight—hikers walk along the edge of the rooms but are not allowed inside. That is not the case at the less-visited Wukoki, Citadel, Nalakihu, and Lomaki ruins. While visitors must be careful not to step on 800-year-old walls, hiking trails lead through tiny doorways and into rooms. The Citadel and Wukoki ruins sit high on top of small plateaus, offering panoramic vistas of the surrounding volcanic craters and Painted Desert. The Citadel is

Exploring a ruin at Wupatki National Monument

especially interesting because its walls are constructed of both sandstone and black lava rock. Its inhabitants may have once lived in fear of nearby Sunset Volcano, which, when they lived on this site, smoked and belched lava.

Sunset Crater Volcano National Monument

Sunset Crater Volcano National Monument protects a 1,000-foot volcanic cone and its surrounding formations. The visitor center is 2 miles from the southern entrance to a loop road off US 89. A stop at the visitor center is important. Hikers learn the type of volcano—a cinder cone—they will see. A video of actual volcanic

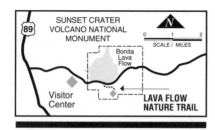

activity helps to both set the stage and illustrate what the crater's volcanic rock looked like in its liquid state. A U.S. Forest Service-managed campground—which fills most summer evenings—is located near the visitor center. Sunset Crater Volcano hikers need a container of drinking water, thick-soled footwear, a hat, a map, and perhaps binoculars.

A lava field at Sunset Volcano National Monument

Lava Flow Nature Trail

1 mile, loop, year-round

This trail is the most popular hike in Sunset Crater Volcano National Monument. Since most children are naturally fascinated by volcanoes and this trail looks intriguing from the start, parents likely will have little trouble generating enthusiasm for the hike. This is a perfect volcano to take kids to because it is so accessible. Within a 1-mile loop, hikers can view the many twisted forms of lava. These include cinders, tubes, squeeze-ups, xenoliths, fumaroles, pahoehoe, and aa. Hikers can view nature at work at the crater by reading trail markers describing the flora of the park and looking for many signs of life around them.

The trail begins at the restrooms. Hikers may purchase a Lava Flow Trail Guide at the visitor center or read the interpretive signs along the trail. The first marker is off the main trail to the right where chunks of limestone called xenoliths have been transported to the spot by the lava flow.

Out on the flat, barely vegetated cinders, visitors learn how the Sinagua people inhabited the area between A.D. 800 and 1100. Proof of their existence has been found under cinders in excavations of pithouses and in the impressions of domesticated corn in the lava itself.

While walking the monument, note that vegetation such as the tall ponderosa pine flourishes where it seems like nothing could exist. Ask your children for a theory. Then allow them to read the brochure for answers.

Ask children to remember the last time they played in the mud. They love the way the stuff oozes through their fingers. Then have them imagine lava doing the same thing as they look at the squeeze-ups. These formations look like the spiky back of a triceratops. Have them find comparable likenesses for other lava forms.

At the next stop, point out that the cinders, with their many holes caused by volcanic gasses, are like styrofoam: great insulators. The ancient Sinaguans appreciated the way the cinders kept the ground from drying out too fast and let the water run down quickly through the top layer. Note the plant succession present in the park.

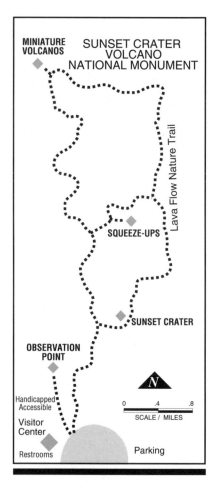

MINIATURE
VOLCANOS

SUNSET CRATER
VOLCANO
NATIONAL MONUMENT

Lava Flow Nature Trail

SQUEEZE-UPS

SUNSET CRATER

OBSERVATION
POINT

Handicapped
Accessible

Visitor
Center

Restrooms

Parking

N

0   .4   .8

SCALE / MILES

The ice cave on the trail at Sunset Crater Volcano is closed because portions of it have collapsed. Hikers may walk through another such cave west of Flagstaff in the Coconino National Forest (see Lava River Cave hike).

The fumarole along the Lava Flow Nature Trail reminds visitors of the hot pots at Yellowstone National Park. Notice the layers of lava built up around the edges.

At the next two stops, hikers learn about different kinds of volcanoes. These include the San Francisco Peaks, which can be seen in the distance and are an example of a composite volcano. Sunset Crater Volcano is a cinder cone volcano.

The next few markers discuss the different forms of lava found at Sunset Crater Volcano and the animals that thrive in this unique environment. After the marker on volcanic forecasting, turn right and continue up a set of metal stairs, over a tall lava flow.

At the Colors of Sunset marker, look down at the deep cracks and compare them with other kinds of cracks. On the way back to the trailhead, take time to turn around and visualize this place as a red and steaming landscape, something it once was and may be again.

Coconino National Forest

This national forest surrounds the Flagstaff area, offering hiking trails, wilderness experiences, and a few good camping alternatives to the often crowded Grand Canyon National Park. The Peaks Ranger District office at 5075 N. Highway 89 in Flagstaff is a good place for families interested in doing longer overnight trips into the wilderness to pick up literature, directions, and detailed hiking maps. Popular Oak Creek Canyon—located south of Flagstaff and north of Sedona—is administered out of the Sedona Ranger District office. For information on Oak Creek Canyon, contact the Sedona Ranger District. The canyon's five campgrounds are extremely popular and fill fast. Advance reservations can be made and are strongly recommended. Two of the more popular family activities in the Flagstaff-Sedona area involve swimming at Slide Rock and Grasshopper Swim Area in Oak Creek Canyon. In fact, they are so popular that parking can sometimes be a problem, so it is good to arrive early in the day. Pets and glass containers are prohibited. These places have the feel of an old swimming hole, making them popular places to let children cool off after hot hikes in the nearby desert. Less crowded wilderness areas are found adjacent to Oak Creek Canyon and near the outskirts of Sedona. Many feature relatively easy hiking experiences. For families looking to enjoy day-long or overnight adventures in the area, the Sedona Ranger District office can provide detailed literature on trails, elevation gains, and lengths of hikes.

Fatman's Loop

2.2 miles, loop, mid-June through September

Families visiting Flagstaff have choices beyond a motel swimming pool or a noisy campground. They can enjoy a delightful

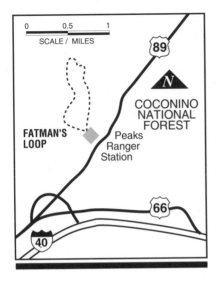

evening or morning hike on Fatman's Loop. The loop trail follows a short tour of the ponderosa pine forest that covers the foothills of volcanic Mount Elden. Hikers experience views of dozens of ancient craters, northern Flagstaff, and a forested plateau.

This trail is part of the Mount Elden trail system, which is also connected to Flagstaff's urban trail network. Located off Highway 89 north of Flagstaff, the hike begins at the Mount Elden trailhead parking area just north of the Coconino Peaks Ranger Station. The parking area is marked with a sign on the west side of US 89.

Although the trail features a few surprises for children, initiate games to keep short legs hiking. An ample supply of pine cones serves as ammunition for a game of "pine cone tag" along the way. Large trees and huge boulders give children excellent hiding places. A "Name that Sound" game will entice youngsters to listen for birds, mammals, and other forest sounds. These hills are alive with the scolding of squirrels, the twitters of birds, and, of course, the utterings of insects.

The trail begins at a slightly uphill grade through cliffrose, ponderosa pine, juniper, and oak. It comes to a crossroads where the hiker must choose which way to begin the loop. The trail to the right leads around the front of the mountain. Its climb is longer but more gradual. The left trail gains most of the elevation quickly but then becomes an easier downhill hike. This description begins with the trail to the right.

The sun warms the lower portion of the trail, leading around boulders with a few ups and downs. Hikers pause at a log fence that limits access to hikers and mountain bikers only. Approximately 0.25 mile later, a sign indicates that hikers are on the right trail, pointing them toward the more difficult Mount Elden Lookout Trail and Fatman's Loop. The trail then enters some healthy stands of

Fatman's Loop near Flagstaff

oak, making it a great place to enjoy fall colors. At a burned-out but still living juniper on the left, the path jumps sharply to the right and then goes uphill again. Hikers must duck under the limbs of a colossal juniper. Look back to see the 3-foot–diameter branch smooth from the youngsters who obviously could not resist the chance to climb this tree or pose for a photo on it.

Be reluctant to feel discouraged or lost. Just as a family wonders if it has become disoriented, the trail starts to turn south back to the parking area. It passes an arroyo to the right and heads back toward the tallest part of the mountain, snaking through trailer-sized boulders.

The trail then gets steeper as it winds through a rock garden of aster and penstemon. Make certain to turn around for a view of Flagstaff's railroad yards and the excavated pit cut into the side of a cinder cone. Gravel comes from this pit and is used to help make the city's snowy streets more passable in the winter months.

A series of switchbacks leads up to the south through a forest scarred by a 1977 wildfire started by a single campfire. Look up at the red and green pinnacles of Mount Elden. At this point, the electronic towers on top of the peak are obscured from view. The trail continues through an oak grove where a hiker has the exalted feeling of being above it all without having to climb the summit. The oak gives way to a drier slope of cliffrose, yucca, and prickly pear and finally to an impressive stand of ponderosa. Here the trail splits. The right fork goes to the Elden Lookout Trail. The view now includes the Painted Desert to the distant east. From here, the descent is relatively quick, with short switchbacks. Enjoy the hike through the oak and ponderosa and look for the sign at the crossroads of Fatman's Loop Trail and the Oldham and Buffalo Park trails. It is a short distance back to the log gate to complete the loop.

Lava River Cave

3,820 feet, one-way, summer and fall

Of all the lava tubes that can be explored in the Four Corners region, Lava River Cave may offer the most in the way of incredible adventure. Imagine leaving the forest and entering a remote, dark cavern that is much colder. By the light of only a flashlight or lantern, hikers explore the twisting, turning 3,820-foot-long cave where temperatures dip as low as 35 degrees Fahrenheit in some places. The place is so cold, in fact, that ice often forms at the bottom. Local legend has it that early settlers actually collected ice from the caves.

To reach Lava River Cave, drive north from Flagstaff 14 miles on State Highway 180, heading toward the South Rim of the Grand Canyon. Turn west on Forest Service Road 245 and travel 3 miles to a fork. Take the fork to the south 1 mile on Forest Service Road 171 and, at a sign that reads 171B, turn east. The trailhead is well marked.

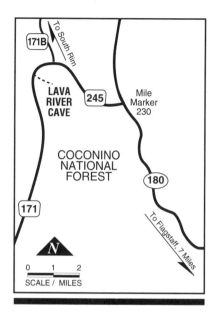

Follow the path to the cave entrance, which requires a short but relatively easy climb downward. Come well prepared to explore a cave, which means carrying at least three sources of light. A pair of battery-powered flashlights coupled with a gas-powered lantern make an excellent combination. If children wonder why they must each carry a flashlight, walk a few hundred yards into the cave and have everyone in the group turn off their lights. Chances are, family members will be amazed at how dark this place can be. Because the lava can be sharp, good hard-soled boots are a must. Temperatures inside the cave range from 35 to 45 degrees Fahrenheit, so it is also a good idea to wear a sweater or jacket. Wearing a hard hat is a good idea, too.

Curious children might ask how a lava cave is formed. According to the U.S. Forest Service, this cave formed in a few hours after a brief volcanic eruption that occurred 650,000 to 700,000 years ago. When lava flowed from the volcano, it cooled on the top and bottom of the flow. But the lava in the middle continued to flow, thus forming a hollow tube. As hikers walk through Lava River Cave—the longest lava tube in Arizona—they can see such different lava features as flow ripples, splashdowns, cooling cracks, and lavasicles.

The cave can be an eerie place. At some places, the ceiling can be as high as 30 feet. At others, it is so narrow that adults will have to duck in order to continue the walk to the end. Though not always obvious, hikers who look closely might see a bat. There are also signs of crickets, beetles, porcupines, and squirrels. According to the Forest Service, heavy use of the cave by humans means animal sightings can be rare.

To enhance a visit to Lava River Cave, pick up an interpretive trail brochure—which contains a map of the interior of the

Entering Lava River Cave

cave—from the Peaks Ranger District in Flagstaff. The forest service asks hikers to pick up litter left by others and not to build fires within the cave.

Long Canyon Trail

2.9 miles, one-way, year-round

Because of their popularity, visiting Sedona and nearby Oak Creek Canyon can be difficult. The number of people enjoying the area makes finding solitude challenging.

Taking this hike in the Red Rocks/Secret Mountain Wilderness northwest of Sedona can solve that problem. This is a relatively easy hike that involves an elevation gain of only 580 feet. It begins in a juniper forest and leads into a forest of ponderosa flanked by red sandstone mountains.

To reach the trailhead, drive west on US 89A from Sedona. Turn north on Dry Creek Road, which eventually turns into Forest Road 152C. Continue on that route. The trailhead, on the west side of

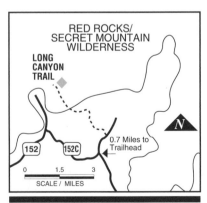

the road, can be picked up just past a fork in the road. Do not turn to the left, but stay on the same paved road for 0.6 mile.

The best part of this wilderness hike is the silence and solitude. Walking through the juniper forest and then into the pines and ultimately into a nice red rock canyon, there is time to think and be still. Children have a little more freedom here and, even in the middle of the day, there is the sense that wildlife is lurking nearby. The place feels wild and alive, as a true wilderness should. Hikers can go for hours without seeing a fellow traveler. This is a good place to pack a lunch.

There are other relatively easy hikes nearby in the Red Rocks/ Secret Mountain Wilderness. Fay Canyon—a 1.1-mile hike—leads to an arch. Vultee Arch, a 1.7-mile trek, and Loy Canyon, an easy 5-mile walk, are all possibilities.

For a detailed map and a list of hikes in Oak Creek Canyon and West Sedona, stop at the Sedona Ranger District office of the Coconino National Forest.

Walnut Canyon National Monument

Walnut Canyon is a 2,249-acre national monument established in 1915. It is open from 8:00 A.M. to 5:00 P.M. year-round except Christmas Day. The entrance road to Walnut Canyon is reached by driving 3 miles off Interstate 40, 7.5 miles east of Flagstaff. For information, write to Superintendent, Walnut Canyon National Monument, Walnut Canyon Road, Flagstaff, AZ 86004. An entrance fee is charged per carload.

Walnut Canyon Island Trail

0.9 mile, loop, year-round but check conditions in winter

The Walnut Canyon Island Trail is easy for older kids who can walk up and down its 240 steps. Children under five may have to

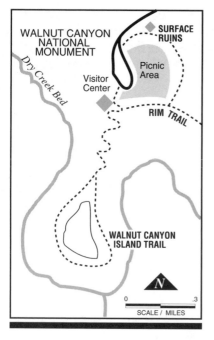

WALNUT CANYON
NATIONAL
MONUMENT

SURFACE
RUINS

Dry Creek Bed

Visitor
Center

Picnic
Area

RIM TRAIL

WALNUT CANYON
ISLAND TRAIL

N

0   .3
SCALE / MILES

be carried or coaxed. Packs for children 35 pounds or less can be borrowed at the visitor center. Because of the steep sides of the trail, all children should be supervised.

From the moment children enter the visitor center, the place captures their imaginations. A look out the window overlooking the canyon will often reveal a turkey vulture gliding above or below the rim. Binoculars attached by wires to a wooden shelf in front of a picture window help children locate cliff dwellings across the canyon. In fact, 100 may be seen from the trail that begins here at the visitor center. It would be a good idea to take binoculars on the trail as well. They help children spot the scattered ruins and abundant wildlife.

Walnut Canyon National Monument protects these cliff dwellings and many rim-top sites of the Sinagua, a people who inhabited the region between 1125 and 1250. Although Sinagua means "without water" in Spanish, nearby Walnut Creek served as a water source for these ancient people. It probably did not flow year-round, but the Sinagua built check dams and terraces. They grew corn, beans, and squash. Signs along the trail identify plants and animals that sustained these ancient people.

The 0.9-mile paved trail begins with a series of steps that help the visitor eventually descend 185 feet. While it is a short hike, it is a natural for children because of the frequent signs either describing ancient life in the canyon or the botanical, historical, and medicinal properties of the plant life utilized by the Sinagua.

Look for the three endangered species that inhabit the canyon. These include the peregrine falcon, Mexican spotted owl, and goshawk. Listen to the gray squirrel identify its territory. Watch for signs of coyote, ring-tailed cat, bobcat, gray fox, cottontail, pack rat, porcupine, or mule deer.

Exploring a Walnut Canyon ruin

Walnut Canyon encourages children to use every sense. Listen to the canyon wren's call as it echoes in the distance. Feel the welcome change in temperature from the heat of the sun to the coolness of the alcoves sheltering the cliff dwellings. Look at centuries-old fingerprints pressed into the mortar. Smell the musky, damp, dusty interiors of the rooms as your eyes adjust to the darkness. Observe that the stones comprising these dwellings are more angular, less perfectly rectangular, than other Southwest dwellings.

Rim Trail

0.75 mile, round-trip,
year-round but check local conditions in winter

After completing the Walnut Canyon Island Trail, take the short Rim Trail. Signs on this trail describe special communities of plants and animals in more detail. At the first turnout, look down for a dead snag and a red-tailed hawk nest. As the trail progresses, differentiate between the pinyon and juniper forest that is away from the canyon's edge on the dry south-facing walls and the wetter, lusher vegetation on north-facing walls. Learn the geology of the canyon.

Looking for birds on a Walnut Canyon trail

Hikers also get a chance to see a pithouse, the prehistoric precursor to the cliff dwellings, and a two-room top-site dwelling, a contemporary of the cliff dwellings. It is not known why some chose to live on the cliffs and others decided to live on top. A mound of rocks of an unexcavated ruin on the trail points out what most of the remaining ruins look like.

Montezuma Castle National Monument

The great Aztec, Montezuma, never heard of this "castle," but about 200 of the Sinagua tribe inhabited the cliff dwellings of this part of Beaver Creek for 300 years. The monument is located just off Interstate 17 at Exit 289. Interpreters have done a good job with strategically placed signs that explain the lifestyle of these desert people.

Montezuma Castle Hike

0.25 mile, one-way, year-round

A wide pathway starting at the visitor center and leading to the well-preserved ruins is shaded by the same tall Arizona sycamore trees that were used as ceiling beams in the original limestone dwellings. After a look at the castle, the trail goes to the right and to Beaver Creek, where the Sinagua agricultural methods are explained. All signs point to the fact that there was food all around. The mystery remains: Where did these people go?

Montezuma Well

0.5 mile, loop, year-round

Montezuma Well is a refreshing and awe-inspiring stop. North of Montezuma Castle, a few miles from Interstate 17 and the McGuireville exit, this "well" was a developed water source for both the Sinagua and Hohokam tribes.

A 0.5-mile paved loop trail starts at the parking lot and goes up a short hill and then down to the rim of a naturally occurring spring. A unique ecosystem is explained here, with the water containing 600 times the normal amount of carbon dioxide.

Montezuma Castle

Farther on, and up a series of stairs, is a warm, subterranean spring that feeds 1.5 million gallons of water a day through a cave in the cliff.

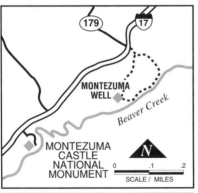

Down a series of stairs to the right, hackberry trees shade the trail. Then, far back under the cliffs, sits an 800-year-old ruin containing seven rooms. Graffiti from the late 1800s is sketched on the walls. From here the water disappears underground.

Hikers may continue the trail to its outlet, where stones and an elaborate irrigation system helped to ensure a steady food supply. Visitors are encouraged to stop here under the velvet ash and sycamore trees, reflect, and cool off in shallow nearby Beaver Creek. The trail on the way back to the parking lot passes the rubble of unexcavated pueblos now overgrown with mesquite, snakeweed, and grasses.

In 1400, the people left an apparently abundant food and water supply and the Verde Valley. Hikers are left to wonder why. Was it disease, internal or external conflicts, or something else that made this happen?

A small ruin near Montezuma Well

Grand Canyon National Park

Located in northern Arizona, the Grand Canyon is the most famous area in the Four Corners region and one of the world's most popular national parks. The major visitor areas are on the south and north rims of the canyon. Though separated by only 10 miles as the crow flies, driving from one rim to the other requires a 215-mile one-way trip. The South Rim, open year-round, is located at an elevation of 7,000 feet above sea level. Summer temperatures average between 50 and 80 degrees Fahrenheit. Winter temperatures range from below 0 to 30 degrees. The North Rim, located at 8,000 feet above sea level, is about 10 degrees cooler. It is open from mid-May to mid-November, depending on the weather.

South Rim. The heavily developed South Rim attracts about 90 percent of the park's annual visitation and is open year-round. The nearest major city is Williams, Arizona. From Flagstaff, the South Rim can be reached by driving northwest on Highway 180 to the town of Valle and then heading north. The South Rim can also be reached by driving west on Highway 64 off US 89 between Page and Flagstaff. With lodging inside and just outside of the park, an airport, and many visitor facilities, the South Rim can accommodate the needs of families with great outdoor experience or those venturing into the outdoors for the first time. Because it hosts hundreds of thousands of visitors with an ancient road system, the South Rim gets crowded. There are times when parking lots at the major overlooks fill.

Reservations for all activities, lodging, and camping are strongly recommended. For example, mule trips into the Grand Canyon are booked up to a year in advance, and some height and weight restrictions apply. Some cancellations do occur, however, so the concessionaire keeps a standby waiting list on a daily basis. Winter mule trips are almost always available. Call 602-638-2401 for reservations.

South Rim and Phantom Ranch inside-the-park lodging is operated by Grand Canyon National Park Lodges. For reservations, call 602-638-2401 or write to Grand Canyon National Park

Taking a break on the South Kaibab Trail

Lodges, Box 699, Grand Canyon, AZ 88023. There is also commercial lodging available just outside the park in Tusayan. Camping—limited to developed facilities—is available at the Mather Campground. Call 1-800-365-2267 or write MISTIX, P.O. Box 85705, San Diego, CA 92186-5705. No hookups are available there, but showers, a laundry, and a dump station are located nearby. The Trailer Village, with hookups, is operated by Grand Canyon National Park Lodges (see above). The Desert View campground, 25 miles east of Grand Canyon Village, furnishes sites on a first-come, first-served basis during the summer months. Private campgrounds as well as U.S. Forest Service facilities are located within an hour's drive of the South Rim. The Lees Ferry Campground—located about halfway between the two rims on the Colorado River—seldom fills and is a great alternative for families shuttling between rims.

Families should consider using a free summer bus shuttle system to get from point to point when visiting the South Rim. One route runs through the village and the other operates on the West Rim (see West Rim Trail below). Because hiking into the

Grand Canyon can be a difficult experience for youngsters, families might consider parking their vehicle at Williams (32 miles west of Flagstaff just off Interstate 40) and taking a 65-mile ride on an old Western steam train. The train runs daily from June through September with a reduced schedule October through May. It departs Williams at 9:30 A.M. and arrives at the Grand Canyon at 11:45 A.M. It departs 3.5 hours later, giving families time to explore some of the overlooks or take a short hike on the ri trail. Overnight options are also available. For reservations, call 1-800-843-8724. Families might also enjoy the IMAX Theater in Grand Canyon Village. River trips on the Colorado—not advisable for younger children—are also available from private outfitters. Advance reservations are strongly recommended. Check at the visitor center for Junior Ranger activities. A special children's newspaper and a number of interpretive activities geared to children's interests are available. Kids are asked to attend interpretive activities and pick up litter in order to earn special patches.

Hiking the Grand Canyon

North Rim. The less-developed North Rim offers food, groceries, lodging, a nice restaurant, camping, and mule trips into the canyon. Families who have not planned ahead might look here first for reservations. The North Rim can be reached by driving southwest on Alternate US 89 from Page, Arizona, and then south from Jacob Lake (lodging, camping, and food available). Kanab, Utah, and Fredonia and Page, Arizona, are the nearest cities. Lodging at the historic Grand Canyon Lodge on the North Rim—built in 1928 by the Utah Parks Company, a subsidiary of the Union Pacific Railroad—is available by writing to TW Recreational Services, Inc., Box 400, Cedar City, UT 84720.

Reservations for the North Rim campground can be obtained by contacting MISTIX, P.O. Box 85705, San Diego, CA 92186–5705, or by calling 1-800-365-2267. Those who do not have a reservation should arrive as early in the day as possible or consider campng at the Jacob Lake facility just outside the park.

Grand Canyon Trail Rides, P.O. Box 128, Tropic, UT 84776, 602-638-2292, schedules 1-day, half-day, and 1-hour mule rides at the North Rim. There is a 12-year-old age limit for a 1-dy trip, an 8-year-old age limit for a half-day trip, and a 6-year-old age limit for the 1-hour rim trip. Weight restrictions also apply to adults. Though reservations are suggested, chances of getting a mule ride on short notice at the North Rim are much greater than on the South Rim.

Grand Canyon Hikes. There is a scene in the movie "Vacation" where a Chicago family on a cross-country journey stops at the edge of the Grand Canyon after driving for days. Looking out at the vast chasm below, the father puts his arm around his wife and says, "Well, kids, there it is. The Grand Canyon." He takes a quick look, sighs, and then herds the family back into its station wagon so it can drive to some other famous sight. Unfortunately, because of the difficulty of some of the hikes into the canyon, that can be the type of Grand Canyon experience many families have. Since the canyon is 277 miles long from Lees Ferry to Grand Wash, there is much to see and do—so much, in fact, that the effort to see the canyon can be downright intimidating to first-time visitors. Hiking into the canyon on trails like Bright Angel, South Kaibab, and North Kaibab is extremely difficult because the trail is so steep and exposed and long. Except for short distances, it is not recommended for younger children. That is why some advance planning for outdoor activities is needed. Because there are a number of short walks to overlooks, have your children take along a nature journal and some colored pencils or crayons. Let them take some time to simply peer into the canyon. Then, allow them to draw or put their feelings into words. Following are four possible hikes, two on each side of the canyon, that allow families to experience the adventure of one of the world's natural wonders.

West Rim Trail

0.25 mile to 8 miles, one-way, year-round, can be icy

Located on the Grand Canyon's South Rim, this might be the best summer hike in the park for families with young children, largely because it affords both a quiet walk and the flexibility to end the hike and pick up a shuttle bus at any time. It can be as short as a 0.3-mile one-way stroll to the first overlook or an all-day 8-mile journey from Bright Angel Lodge to Hermit Trailhead. During the summer months, the paved road that runs parallel to the West Rim Trail is closed to automobile traffic. Free shuttle busses that run from 7:30 A.M. to sunset at approximately 15-minute intervals stop at eight different major overlooks. Families can hike 0.5 mile from the trailhead to Trailview Overlook,

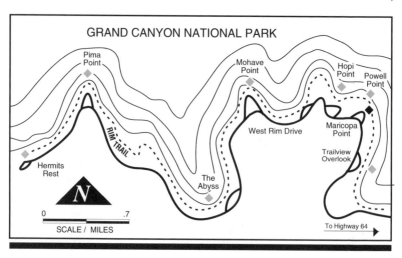

another 0.7 mile to Maricopa Point (where the trail turns from pavement to dirt), another 0.5 mile to Powell Point and the Powell Memorial, and another 0.33 mile to Hopi Point. From there, hikers can walk 0.8 mile to Mohave Point, 1.1 miles to the Abyss, 2.9 miles to Pima Point, and another 1.1 mile to Hermits Rest. Throughout the length of the hike, there is only a 200-foot elevation gain. The beauty of this trail is that it provides fabulous views of the canyon, comparative solitude in contrast to other places on the South Rim where automobile traffic is allowed, and flexibility. When the kids get tired or bored, a family can simply end the hike at the next shuttle stop and take the bus to the next overlook or back to the trailhead.

When starting at Bright Angel Lodge, the first overlook gives hikers a glimpse of the many switchbacks of the Bright Angel Trail, which leads down into the canyon. Gnarled old juniper trees and ancient sagebrush can be viewed along the way.

At the Trailview Overlook, about 0.5 mile into the trip, kids must scramble down a series of stairs that leads to an overlook. That is typical of all the overlooks, which offer spectacular views of the canyon below coupled with informative interpretive signs.

During much of the rim hike, the rock formations known as Cheops Pyramid and Buddha Temple are visible in the canyon. Have your kids come up with some of their own names for the formations. Hikers with good eyes can peer out across the 10-mile-wide canyon and get a glimpse of the North Rim Lodge.

Walking farther along the rim, hikers reach Plateau Point, where they can see Bright Angel Canyon, Indian Garden, Inner Gorge, Brahma Temple, Zoroaster Temple, Cape Royal, and Yavapai Point.

At about this point in the trail, an old mine will come into sight, looking strangely out of place in the midst of the colorful wild wonder of the Grand Canyon. The Orphan Mine—with its large tram—operated until 1969, producing copper, uranium, silver, and vanadium. In 1951, it was America's main source of uranium.

At times, the West Rim Trail is so close to the road that hikers can see busses zipping past noisily. At other times, it moves out next to the edge of the canyon. Because of steep dropoffs, parents should keep a wary eye on their children. The farther away from the trailhead a family ventures, the more chances there are for solitude. Unlike the major hikes into the canyon or the overlooks where cars are allowed, it is possible to find solitude on this trail.

Those who make it all the way to Hermits Rest, either by foot or by bus, can stop for a cold drink, sandwich, or ice cream cone at the small snack bar. Another trail—a strenuous 5-mile round-trip adventure with a 1,200-foot change in elevation—begins at this point.

South Kaibab Trail to Cedar Ridge

3 miles, round-trip, year-round

Families with young children will have a difficult time passing up the adventure involved in hiking down into the Grand Canyon. Looking at switchbacking trails that hug cliffs and lead into different types of rocks and geologic formations will entice many to try at least a short walk into the canyon. The rewards are great, and for young hikers getting their first taste of a real challenge the feeling of accomplishment at the end of the trail is wonderful.

Perhaps the best such hike is the 3-mile round-trip trek along the South Kaibab Trail to Cedar Ridge, a strenuous trek that leads 940 feet down into the canyon from the South Kaibab trailhead just before Yaki Point off the East Rim Drive. One thing is guar-

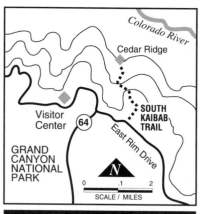

anteed. Families who make this trek will not forget it and will quickly gain an appreciation for the scale and size of the Grand Canyon, though they are nowhere near making the hike all the way to the bottom.

Despite the difficulty, young children can and do make this trip and, at times, seem to enjoy it more than their parents. Especially on hot days, though, it will require

A rugged Grand Canyon trail

some coaxing. That is why the best advice for families who decide to attempt this hike is to start as early in the day as possible. The National Park Service recommends not hiking on this trail between 10:00 A.M. and 4:00 P.M. in the summer months. Getting up before sunrise and driving to the trailhead east of the South Rim visitor center and Mather Point helps a family of hikers beat the heat, avoid large crowds, and enjoy the early morning colors of a Grand Canyon sunrise. Temperatures are cooler at this time of day, making the hike down a pleasant one and the hike back up much easier than in the middle of the afternoon under a scorching desert sun when the plentiful mule manure on the trail begins to stink and draw flies.

Speaking of mules, trail etiquette calls for hikers to yield the trail to mules. Where it is too narrow for human and mule, hustle to the nearest spot where the animals and their riders can pass.

More than any other hike listed in this book, the South Kaibab Trail requires advance preparation. Bring plenty of water—rangers recommend carrying two to three quarts of water per person—and some snack foods for energy, and wear good hiking boots. Also, because restrooms are scarce along the open trail, it is best to encourage children to relieve themselves before starting the hike.

The hike down is deceptively easy. Though the trail feels like a slippery slide in spots where there is loose gravel, footing is solid. But there are some steep dropoffs along the way, and parents need to keep their children under control and well supervised.

Look for cliffrose and juniper growing out of unlikely spots in the cliffs where enough water and soil have combined to allow a semblance of life. Notice that the colors and textures of the rock change every few hundred yards. Turn the hike into an educational experience by picking up at the visitor center a brochure or guidebook that helps identify the different layers of rock that can be seen as you walk down into the canyon.

When hikers reach Cedar Ridge, they can walk out to a peninsula-like formation with dropoffs on both sides. Find a quiet spot along the trail where you can sit and look at the canyon below while gathering energy for the long trip back to the rim. This is a good time to grab a quick, energy-producing snack.

When walking back to the rim, do not be afraid to take plenty of breaks. There are rocks and wide spots in the trail that make convenient rest stops. To break the monotony of the uphill hike, parents might have their children count the number of switchbacks, sing songs, or tell stories.

Reaching the rim to complete the 3-mile round-trip hike is quite an accomplishment for a young hiker. Celebrate by heading to one of the lodges for a malt, ice cream cone, or lunch.

A view from South Kaibab Trail

Uncle Jim's Trail

5 miles, round-trip, May 15–October 31 most years

Begin this North Rim hike at the North Kaibab trailhead 2 miles north of the Grand Canyon Lodge. The best thing about this hike is that it can be enjoyed at almost any time of day, largely because it winds its way through an alpine forest of ponderosa and aspen. The shade of the trees offers hikers a cool respite from the hotter, more exposed areas on the canyon rims.

Early in the morning, as wranglers get their mules ready at the trailhead for a day's work, hikers might get glimpses of wildlife. Mule deer, squirrels, and an occasional wild turkey can be sighted along the way. Take time to sit on a log and simply listen to the sounds of the forest. If children enjoy searching for birds, bring along a pair of binoculars and a bird guidebook. Chances are, there will be plenty of birds to spot and identify.

An early morning ride is one of the best ways to experience the Grand Canyon's North Rim.

The trail leads to Uncle Jim's Point, offering a beautiful view of the Grand Canyon below. There is little elevation gain along the way, making this an easy and enjoyable half-day walk that, though slightly longer than many trails for young children, presents a chance to experience the sights and sounds of the forest.

Bright Angel Point

0.5 mile, round-trip, May 15–October 31 most years

This North Rim hike is a self-guided nature trail. Start it at either the log shelter near the Grand Canyon Lodge or from the east patio behind the lodge.

Since this is one of the most popular hikes on the North Rim, expect to find people walking the slightly steep incline to the point at all times of the day. However, this is not an altogether unpleasant experience. Have your children sit and listen to the different languages they will hear as they walk along the paved trail. This truly is a way to experience an international park. Talk to your

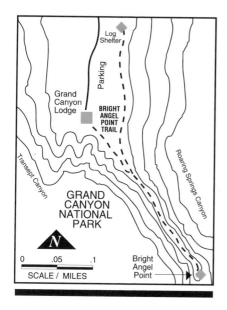

children about the concept of a national park and the special qualities of places like the Grand Canyon and what they mean to the people of the world.

At the end of the trail, hikers are rewarded with a panoramic view of the deep canyon gorge. On clear days, it is possible to look 10 miles across to the South Rim. If you have a good geology guide, identify the different types of rock layers that have been cut over millions of years by the Colorado River, located far below.

Glen Canyon National Recreation Area

Lake Powell, the huge reservoir that is the heart of the Glen Canyon National Recreation Area, is 186 miles long with 1,960 miles of shoreline. It is formed by the Glen Canyon Dam in Arizona and includes the area of the Colorado River from the dam to Lees Ferry, where the Grand Canyon begins. Administered by the National Park Service, it is one of the Southwest's most popular tourist destinations. Boaters and hikers love to explore its many interesting side canyons and enjoy the reservoir's deep blue water contrasted with towering sandstone cliffs. Though the dam and the huge Wahweap Marina complex of boat docks, service stations, lodges, gift shops, and restaurants is located in Arizona, much of the reservoir—including the main access to Rainbow Bridge

Houseboating on Lake Powell

National Monument—is in Utah. Major marinas, where water-skiing boats or houseboats can be rented, are at Wahweap in Arizona and Bullfrog, Hite, and Hall's Crossing in Utah. There are lodging facilities at Bullfrog and Wahweap and campgrounds at all marinas but Dangling Rope. This is a boater's paradise, with many bays and plenty of beaches. Fishing for striped bass, smallmouth bass, and largemouth bass can be excellent. Kids especially enjoy fishing for easy-to-catch bluegill, bullheads, carp, and channel catfish. There is also a nice campground at Lees Ferry, which serves as a place to spend the night for families traveling from the South to the North rim of the Grand Canyon.

One of the most popular family activities at Lake Powell involves renting a houseboat for three days to a week and heading out on the reservoir, camping on red sand beaches, swimming, and exploring. Another less expensive alternative involves renting a smaller 16- or 18-foot powerboat and packing camping equipment in the bow. Gasoline can be obtained at the Dangling Rope Marina near Rainbow Bridge about 40 miles up reservoir from the dam. Families without boats can tour Lees Ferry downstream from the dam or learn about the Colorado River Storage Project by visiting the Carl Hayden Visitor Center next to the Glen Canyon Dam. The visitor center's many detailed informational displays on dam building on the Colorado River System educate about Western water management. Tours of the Glen Canyon Dam also start at the visitor center. Families would do well to take such a tour. Children can learn how flowing water helps generate electricity, view the control room of the power plant, and learn about the difficulties in building a dam in this desolate country. Nearby Page, Arizona, has motel, grocery store, and restaurant facilities.

Lees Ferry Nature Trail

1 mile, one-way, year-round

This short walk along the Colorado River is also a walk back in history. It is a good morning or evening hike since there is little shade afforded by trees or outcroppings. Remains of pioneer buildings and Lees Ferry are found along the trail. A trail brochure may be picked up at the Carl Hayden Visitor Center near the dam and, at times, near the trailhead. The trail starts upriver from the boat ramp. It reveals details of the history of this scenic and tiny ghost town. The stones for the building's walls, 1.5 feet thick, were quarried not far away.

Lees Ferry on the Colorado River resembles a ghost town.

This ferry was once bustling with pioneers, their wagons, and stock, on their way across the Colorado River to points south in Arizona. Originally started by Mormon pioneer John D. Lee in 1871, the ferry remained an important passage point for years. Lee was later executed for his part in the Mountain Meadow Massacre, an infamous event in Mormon history that took place in southwestern Utah. His wife continued to operate the ferry after his death. It was sold and resold to different entities including the Mormon Church, Grand Canyon Cattle Company, and Coconino County in Arizona.

These days, shouts from boaters and rafters echo up from the river, as this is a good place to begin or end river trips. It also serves as a major boat launch for anglers fishing for the feisty large trout that reside in the clear waters of Glen Canyon below the Glen Canyon Dam.

The broad trail leads past rusty machinery. It cuts down through a wash and up the other side. At stop 6, hikers get a good overview of the Colorado River. The trail continues to another stone house and returns the same way, featuring views of Glen Canyon and the start of the Grand Canyon. It is a quiet place for an evening stroll when the setting sun turns the canyon cliffs crimson and fish can be seen jumping in the green waters of the Colorado River below.

Rainbow Bridge National Monument

There was a time when visiting the world's largest natural bridge involved a grueling 14-mile one-way backpack or horseback ride from nearby Navajo Mountain. The construction of the Glen Canyon Dam changed all that, making the natural bridge relatively easy to access by boat.

The boat ride from Wahweap Marina in Arizona or Hall's Crossing or Bullfrog in Utah to a courtesy dock near the entrance to the bridge is about 50 miles long. Those who do not own boats can take a tour boat from Wahweap, Hall's Crossing, or Bullfrog, which is also an easy way to see the beauty of Lake Powell and the canyon country that surrounds it. At the Dangling Rope Marina, located 10 miles from Rainbow Bridge, boat fuel, supplies from a small store, and restroom facilities are available. The boat ride is a long one and, chances are, most powerboaters will need gasoline to get them back to one of the other marinas.

A short, easy walk leads from the courtesy dock to Rainbow Bridge. The bridge, formed by water breaking through red Navajo sandstone, spans 275 feet and is 290 feet high. After spending time on the boat, children may want to stretch their legs while exploring the area around one of the world's natural wonders.

Pipe Spring
National Monument

Pipe Spring National Monument is located 14 miles west of Fredonia, Arizona, and 36 miles east of Hurricane, Utah. It is a preserved cattle ranch that utilized a natural spring. In this sense, it is an oasis in the flat, dry expanse between the Vermillion Cliffs, Kaibab Plateau, and the Grand Canyon—an area known as the Arizona Strip. Admission is charged for those over 16 and under 62. Historic buildings close at 4:00 P.M. The rest of the monument, including the interpretive trail, closes at 4:30 P.M. There is a snack bar and gift shop at the visitor center and a small private campground on the Paiute Reserve, 0.25 mile on the right, north of the monument. Cowboys and Indians are the stuff of many children's dreams. If they are not, they will be after a visit to this waystop on the trail through the Southwest.

There are three springs here. They were used by the Basketmaker and Pueblo Indians and later by the Paiutes who camped here in their yearly migrations. The Paiutes still live in the area. The monument is located in the Kaibab Paiute Reserve, near the town of Red Hills.

The first ranchers, Dr. James Whitmore and Robert McIntyre, settled Pipe Spring in 1863. They were killed in 1867 by both bullets and arrows. It is uncertain who murdered them. Settlers stayed away for four years. Explorer John Wesley Powell and Mormon missionary Jacob Hamblin signed a treaty between the Mormon Church and the Navajo Nation in 1870 at Fort Defiance, and in September of 1870, Mormon church leader Brigham Young, Hamblin, Powell, and others met at Pipe Spring to discuss turning Pipe Spring into the church's southern Utah tithing ranch. Joseph W. Young initiated the construction, but Anson Perry Winsor oversaw construction of the fort that now sits on the site. It was also known as "Winsor Castle." Many of the Mormons who lived at Pipe Spring earned their living by raising cattle. They also produced cheese and butter that were packed in barrels, insulated with flour, and sent in wagons twice a month to St. George, Utah.

A visit to Pipe Spring starts at the visitor center. Walk out the door for a tour of the ranch. A 0.5-mile loop trail starts north of the pond and west of the fort. Before starting the walk, take

"Winsor Castle" at Pipe Spring National Monument

time to visit the ranch. The rooms of the fort have a lived-in air to them. Thick sandstone walls keep rooms cool.

Pipe Spring Loop Trail

0.5 mile, loop, year-round

The loop trail starts at Pipe Spring itself. There is a trail sign north of the pond. The trail continues with a trail marker pointing out a telegraph line strung on a gnarled juniper pole, describing how the telegraph was welcomed to Pipe Spring in 1871 because it could increase communication to this area and perhaps announce the danger of impending Indian raids, which never actually materialized.

Several short switchbacks cut through the red-orange Chinle sandstone and red prickly pear cactus. Partway, note how rock for the two-foot-thick walls of the fort was quarried from this hillside.

Next, stop for a breath and imagine the arid Arizona Strip as a lush, ungrazed prairie with grass as high as a horse's belly. Overgrazing by cattle left it an inhospitable desert.

The stop before the top explains the uppermost sandstone formation, which is called the Navajo formation. For a good view of the lands surrounding the Arizona Strip, walk on a ledge to the top along this common Southwestern rock formation.

The top of the hill also has markers detailing the flora of the pinyon/juniper forest. A distinctive plant, easy for kids to identify, is the silvery rounded leaf of the buffaloberry. Its tart orange berries were collected by pioneers to make into pastries and jellies. Remind children that the plants are part of the national monument and cannot be picked.

Stop, too, at the sign that identifies the major landmarks of the vast expanse. Of interest is the campsite of the Franciscan explorers Dominguez and Escalante who stopped within 8 miles of Pipe Spring. Visible to the east is the Kaibab Paiute Indian Reservation, home to less than 500 today.

Walk over the flat top of the hill and down the back side to get an overview of the ranch. The trail ends up behind the fort that, from this angle, appears to be a split-level home. Stay awhile, perhaps, in the unhurried atmosphere of an uncrowded park and chat with rangers well versed in the region's history.

Petrified Forest National Park

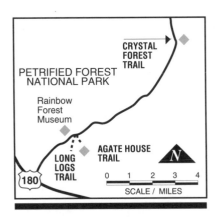

Located off Interstate 40 east of Holbrook, Arizona, this park features the Southwest's famed Painted Desert as well as acres of petrified wood and some scattered ancient ruins. With a restaurant, gift shop, and service station located near the north entrance off Interstate 40 and a gift shop and soda shop near the south entrance off US 180, this is a relatively easy park for families to explore. There is, however, no camping and no lodging inside the park. Only backpackers with overnight permits who want to access the many acres of wilderness within Petrified Forest National Park can spend the night. They will need to obtain a free permit from the visitor center. Most of the trails off the park's only road are easily enjoyed by young hikers. Remind youngsters to resist the temptation to collect petrified wood in the park. If everyone who visited the park took just a small piece home, there soon would not be much for visitors to see. Be advised, too, that there is a good chance your car will be checked by a ranger as you leave the park. Park roads and trails close in the evening, so check the hours they are open at the entrance station or visitor center at either end of the park road.

Crystal Forest Trail

0.8 mile, loop, year-round

Imagine a Triassic Age scene in this dry desert climate. Tall, pine-like trees live in the headwaters of a broad floodplain. Dinosaurs roam the land. Today you can view their remains in the form of petrified wood on this easy paved loop in the south-central region of the park. The trailhead is accessed right off the main park road.

There is no shortage of logs today in this desert forest. They have simply turned from wood to stone. They have petrified over millions of years lying in silt, mud, and volcanic ash, with the wood slowly replaced by silica deposited from the groundwater.

Logs 3 and 5 feet in diameter litter the trail. So do exploded logs. Before this area became a park, some of these ancient trees were dynamited so commercial miners could obtain purple amethyst, clear quartz, and smoky quartz crystals. Have children distinguish all the colors striping the cross-sections of the wood. Challenge them to find words to describe the tall logs lying in slices like some ancient reptile's giant vertebrae. Let them feel the surface that looks so alive and compare it with its living counterpart.

Hiking in Petrified Forest National Park

Agate House and Long Logs Trails

0.5 mile each, loop, year-round

These trails begin at the same parking lot in the southern-most region of the park near the south entrance. Each trail consists of a 0.5-mile loop with Long Logs on the north and Agate House on the south.

Agate House can be seen in the distance after the beginning of the trail, which wanders through forests of prone petrified wood. Complete logs, smaller chunks, and tiny pebbles litter the route. Although small by the standard of many Southwest Anasazi ruins, Agate House itself is a wonder. The ancient people who built this home were known for using all available materials. Here, that meant using petrified wood, making this a colorful, highly sturdy dwelling. This reconstructed pueblo may rank as the most colorful in the entire Four Corners area. Have children peek inside, comparing the wooden beams of the roof with the petrified wood walls.

The Long Logs trail is an easy walk that gives hikers plenty of opportunity to study petrified wood. There is more petrified wood on this walk than in any other part of the park. This is an especially beautiful hike early in the day or near sunset. Examine the sparkling cross-sections of wood. Measure the longest logs. Count how many trees there are per square yard of land. Toward the north end of the loop trail, look north at dozens of logs, mostly intact, and trunks scattered over the gray and mauve clay in the distance.

Hikers also get a chance to see a log that is breaking into tiny pieces, a close-up example of how weathering works to reduce these giants to mere fragments. Let children use a magnifying glass to get a closer look at the logs along the trail. It is extremely tempting to take just a small souvenir home from this trail, so have children look at this log carefully and ask them to calculate how many visitors enjoy this trail each day and how many days it would take before the entire log would be gone. This little lesson underscores the basic mission of the National Park Service, which is to protect priceless natural resources, allow natural processes to continue, and give visitors a chance to enjoy the park at the same time. The only reason the logs exist is because someone had the foresight to set this site aside as a national park. Thus, instead of collecting a sample, collect a memory.

Canyon de Chelly National Monument

Located in the heart of the remote Navajo Indian Reservation, Canyon de Chelly can be reached by driving on US 191 to Chinle and then east on Arizona Highway 7. Management of this 83,840-acre monument is an interesting mix combining the skills of the National Park Service with the Navajo Tribe. Because of that, only one trail—the White House Ruin—can be hiked without a Navajo guide. There are a number of overlooks that can be enjoyed from the road as well. Hiring a Navajo guide might involve a hike or a four-wheel-drive or horseback ride into the canyon ruins, complete with an interesting interpretation of the natural landscape. Campers can stay at a large campground guarded by huge cottonwood trees. Thunderbird Lodge is located inside the monument, and there are two motels just outside the park. Reservations are suggested during the busy summer months. Check out the Navajo hogan and the video at the visitor center where, during the summer months, a Navajo silversmith shows how to make jewelry. The monument also offers a Junior Ranger program.

White House Ruin

2.5 miles, round-trip, spring–fall

Variety makes the trek to White House Ruin a special trip, but one best enjoyed in the off-season or early in the day before the canyon heats up. The trail leads to impressive ruins, one built at the level of the small wash at the bottom of the canyon and others constructed in a cliff alcove.

Begin the trail at the White House Overlook parking area. Follow trail markers and skirt the edge of the cliff until a dugout through the sandstone curves around and begins a steady descent down the cliff face. This whole downward climb, in fact, is literally carved from rocks. In two places, hikers walk through tunnels,

The White House Ruin at Canyon de Chelly

a part of the trail sure to delight children. The switchbacks afford many views of the canyon and the pastoral scene below of a Navajo farm. Avoid taking pictures or walking into the farm. This is someone's home, and it should be respected.

In the morning sun, hikers' shadows dance upon the vertical rock walls that border the trail. Imagine these shadows as Kachinas or as ancient people making their way to the canyon floor and the cool waters of the welcoming river. Going through the final tunnel feels a bit like Alice going through the looking glass. At the exit, a Navajo hogan—a traditional round home—greets visitors. So do cultivated fields and the smell of horses. Farming has continued in this valley floor in much the same manner since A.D. 1040. Though the ancient people have disappeared, the Navajo people now farm this canyon.

Turn the corner to the left and continue hiking through a barrier of Russian olive and tamarisk trees. These exotic species from the Eastern hemisphere have invaded the river system and often choke out native species.

Once at the bottom, look up and figure out where the trail actually led off the sheer sandstone cliff. Ask children how they think ancient people reached the canyon floor.

The trail continues along in deep sand and soon joins a four-wheel-drive road that is used by Navajo guides and Thunderbird Lodge on a regular basis to reach the ruin. Another good reason to hike early is that it helps avoid the noise of the vehicles and the larger crowds that reach the ruin at the middle of the day. The stream must be crossed here. Its depth varies with the weather and time of year. In the spring, hikers will likely have to take off their boots and wade across. In the hot summer months, the river retreats to little more than a small creek that is easily crossed.

A tall fence keeps hikers from attempting to climb the cliff to the alcove and the dwelling. Some of these ruins are well preserved

One of Arizona's many fine visitor centers

because of their placement back under the alcove. The ruin gets its name because one of the dwellings is covered with a white plaster, an unusual sight in the Southwest. The thick walls are constructed in the Chacoan style of building. The small windows, like eyes, peer out across the canyon. One wonders how much the scene has changed over the centuries.

Colorado

More than any one reason, families visit southern Colorado to enjoy the mountains. This is a land dominated by rocky, snow-capped peaks. Big peaks. While most families will not scale the summit of one of Colorado's 14,000-foot mountains, they certainly will enjoy the view as they ride an old narrow-gauge steam train, walk an alpine trail, saddle up a horse, or drive past old mining towns turned resorts such as Silverton or Telluride.

In the winter, families flock to ski areas such as Telluride or Purgatory near Durango. During the summer months, they use lifts to carry their mountain bikes up the peaks for explorations of backcountry trails. A child might delight in riding an alpine slide, visiting an old Main Street ice cream parlor, or listening to the whistle of a lonely train.

The simple pleasures of watching a beaver work on a high alpine pond, fishing a pristine mountain stream, or taking a mountain hike to a waterfall bring families from all over the world to southern Colorado where the San Juan and Sangre de Cristo mountains dominate the landscape.

There are, of course, other pleasures. Mesa Verde National Park's cliff dwellings—most easily accessible—offer families a fascinating glimpse at the past. Dinosaurs once roamed the barren deserts of western Colorado near the Utah border. Now families can visit active dinosaur fossil quarries and participate in a dig. Nearby, in the deserts near Grand Junction, families can look down upon sandstone monoliths at Colorado National Monument. Great Sand Dune National Monument's fascinating mixture of sand and mountain wilderness provides children with a gigantic playground and adults with a chance to learn more about the area's geology.

No matter where a family travels in southern Colorado, one thing is certain. There will be a range of high mountain peaks nearby.

Grand Junction

Located at the junction of Interstate 70 and US 50 on the edge of the fabled Colorado River, Grand Junction is western Colorado's largest city. The city serves as a base for trips to Colorado National Monument, the Black Canyon of the Gunnison, or the Grand Mesa, a 10,000-foot alpine wonderland full of pristine lakes.

The town itself contains some interesting possibilities for family activities. Kids who enjoy seeing dinosaurs usually like visiting the life-like moving reptiles in the Dinosaur Valley exhibit at 362 Main Street. The new Devils Canyon Science Center located near Dinosaur Hill in Fruita west of Grand Junction also features many hands-on exhibits children will enjoy. Some planned activities include family digs for real dinosaur bones as part of package tours.

Children should also enjoy a visit to the Doo Zoo Children's Museum at 635 Main Street. The Cross Orchards Historic Site at 3079 F Road displays a living history exhibit of what life was like on an orchard in the 1900s. The Fun Junction Amusement Park at 2878 North Avenue, a swimming pool and waterslide at Lincoln Park, and the Bookcliff Exotic Animal Park are pleasant diversions for families on hot summer days after young feet get tired from walking desert trails.

Rabbit Valley

This Bureau of Land Management area is located 2 miles east of the Utah border and 30 miles west of Grand Junction just off Interstate 70. The Museum of Western Colorado in nearby Grand Junction and Dinamation Discovery Expeditions help administer it. Pit toilets, but no water, are available.

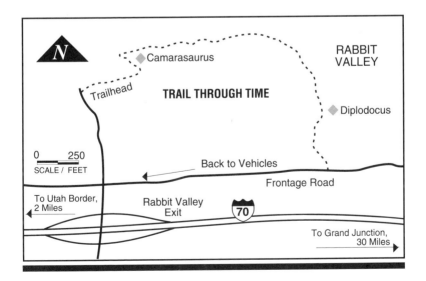

Trail Through Time

1.5 miles, loop, year-round

Want to let your children explore a real Jurassic Park? Then this is the place. This moderately strenuous self-guided interpretive loop trail takes hikers back 140 million years to a time when dinosaurs roamed this area. Instead of today's dry, sparse landscape, hikers should imagine this place as a lush flood plain.

An information kiosk explains the work being done on site. Many times throughout the year—especially in summer—active digs take place. Families can participate in some of this work by contacting Dinamation Discovery Expeditions in nearby Fruita about their paleontology expeditions. Informative bronze plaques with text and graphics mark all of the stops along the trail. A wheelchair-accessible trail leads from the parking lot to the kiosk and quarry.

The quarry near the first trail marker appears to have been a watering hole where plant-eating dinosaurs became dinner for meat-eaters. Scientists have uncovered Camarasaurus, Diplodocus, and Allosaurus bones here.

Continue on the trail to see how dinosaur bones look while still embedded in rock. At the second stop, up a short switchback, look for something resembling gray x's. These are the neck vertebrae and front limb bone of a Camarasaurus.

The trail leads slightly uphill. A bench soon appears where hikers can enjoy a break while looking out over the desolate plateau to the pointed La Sal Mountains near Moab, Utah.

The climb continues a short distance before slowly descending back to a frontage road that leads back to the parking area. Hikers who make the entire climb are rewarded by seeing clearly visible vertebrae of a Diplodocus, an 80-foot-long dinosaur that once roamed the area. Fun, too, are the large yellow-headed collared lizards that can be seen in good numbers during the summer. Can your children make the connection between these reptiles and their distant relatives, the dinosaurs, that roamed here thousands of years ago?

Watch closely for arrows pointing to the correct trail after Marker 10 on the self-guided loop because additional unmarked trails take off in different directions. A dropoff on a dry waterfall near one of these side trails could be dangerous for younger children.

Colorado National Monument

Located off Highway 340 in Western Colorado between the towns of Fruita and Grand Junction, a scenic 23-mile paved road connects the east (Grand Junction) and west (Fruita) entrances to this colorful national monument. The visitor center, spacious campground, and picnic area are located near the west entrance. Another picnic area can be found near the east entrance, water and modern restrooms in the campground and visitor center. Camping spaces are almost always available. A number of short trails, one self-guided, make this an excellent family vacation destination. The visitor center offers a good Junior Ranger program.

Window Rock Nature Trail

0.5 mile, round-trip,
year-round, could be impassable in winter

Located on the west end of the campground near a covered overlook, this easy route provides a good introduction to the monument after families set up camp. It leads to a covered viewpoint with views of Wedding Canyon and the agricultural valley of the Colorado River. Watch your children closely. There are some unfenced dropoffs on this trail.

Ottos Trail

1 mile, round-trip,
year-round, could be impassable in winter

Named after the monument's first superintendent—John Otto—this out-and-back trail starts with what appears at first to be a gentle walk through a pinyon/juniper forest. Soon, however, hikers are rewarded with views of the red sandstone canyon country below. The final destination is a fenced overlook perched on

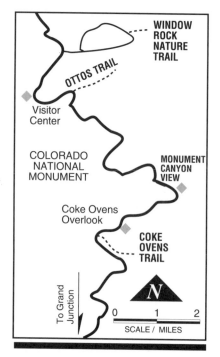

the edge of a cliff. From this point, hikers can enjoy views of tall monoliths as well as Window Rock. Children may be thrilled with the fact that they are walking on a small island of land, about 30 feet wide in most places, with dropoffs and views on both sides.

Coke Ovens

1 mile, one-way, year-round, but can be icy in winter

This trail explores some of the most diverse scenery found in the monument's many short trails. It begins near the middle of the park on the Monument Canyon Trail, a good all-day 12-mile hiking adventure for families with older children looking to spend more time exploring the monument. The two trails start at the same place but split about 200 yards into the hike.

Hikers enjoying a view at Colorado National Monument

The narrow trail winds its way down through red rock, ultimately reaching formations known as the Coke Ovens. These are rounded, tall sandstone spires that resemble ovens. The overlook is fenced.

While walking, look closely at the sides of nearby cliffs to find small "jug handle" arches. Parents must keep close track of their children on this trail. There are steep dropoffs in several places.

Black Canyon of the Gunnison National Monument

Just looking at a map, most families might think the Black Canyon of the Gunnison cannot contain the kind of short, easy walks children enjoy. After all, this 12-mile black gorge is 1,150 feet wide with a depth of 1,725 feet in places. But the monument's south and north rims include a surprising number of easy hikes and nature trails. On the south rim, trails such as the Rim Rock, Cedar Point, and Warner Point nature trails feature short hikes that most children will be able to negotiate. All are under 2 miles round trip. On the north rim, short treks of 3 miles or under can be found on the Chasm View Nature Trail and the first portion of the North Vista Trail. There are a number of shorter strolls to overlooks with views into the immense canyon below. The trails lead through a pinyon/juniper forest. The highest point of the park is 8,289 feet above sea level. Campgrounds on the north and south rims are primitive but nice, offering shaded spots in juniper forests. To reach the south rim of the park from Montrose, drive east on US 50 and then north on Colorado 347. The south rim visitor center is 15 miles from Montrose. To reach the north rim, park rangers tell visitors to use either US 50 east and Colorado 92 west through Curecanti National Recreation Area to Crawford, or US 50 west and Colorado 92 east through Delta to Crawford. From Crawford, a graveled county road leads to the north rim. Access on the north is limited by snow during the winter. Backcountry permits required to backpack into the gorge must be obtained at the south rim visitor center.

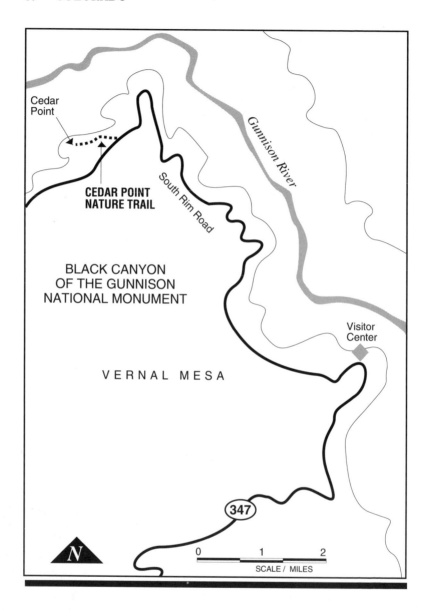

Cedar
Point

**CEDAR POINT
NATURE TRAIL**

South Rim Road

Gunnison River

BLACK CANYON
OF THE GUNNISON
NATIONAL MONUMENT

Visitor
Center

VERNAL MESA

347

N

0   1   2
SCALE / MILES

Cedar Point Nature Trail

0.66 mile, one-way, spring–fall

When hiking in national parks or monuments with steep dropoffs—and there are many such places in the Southwest—safety can be a major consideration for parents. That is why trails such as this relatively safe walk are so inviting.

As it winds its way through a pinyon/juniper forest, wooden markers on the trail describe the animals, plants, and geology. This gives parents plenty of chances to ask children to identify the special characteristics of similar-looking plants like serviceberry, mountain mahogany, and snowberry. Parents seeking to turn this hike into a learning experience can assign each family member a specific plant. On later hikes in the trip, ask the child to identify his or her special plant.

The trail leads to two fenced areas with good views of the Gunnison River 2,000 feet below. The Painted Wall—a 2,300-foot cliff that is Colorado's tallest—sits across the canyon. Take time to allow children to quietly contemplate the earth's power. The wide, lighter bands of rock streaking the canyon walls are composed of volcanic material, pushed up through fractures in the surrounding rock, that subsequently hardened.

Looking down on the Black Canyon of the Gunnison

Curecanti National Recreation Area

Located east of the Black Canyon of the Gunnison on US 50, Curecanti is primarily a boater's park and includes several large reservoirs, marinas, and campground complexes, but there are activities for hikers as well. Families can choose between longer 4-mile hikes or short walks along fishing access trails. Those in the mood for a longer day hike will enjoy the Dillon Pinnacles, a fairly level trail that leads up a dry mesa to the rock pinnacles that give the place its name. Views of Blue Mesa Reservoir are also impressive.

Neversink Trail

1.5 miles, round-trip,
spring–fall, intermittently in winter

Located on the eastern edge of the national recreation area, this short trail does not look like much at first. But for families willing to stop, look, listen, and quietly walk its level, graveled trail, there can be great rewards. With a restroom facility and picnic tables at the trailhead, Neversink offers traveling families a good place for a short half-hour to 1-hour walk and a break from a long drive.

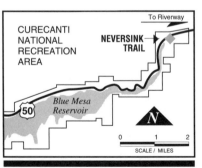

Search the clear Gunnison River for signs of trout darting in and out of deep holes in shallower portions of the river. Look for shy mule deer quietly grazing in the high grass across the river. Bring a pair of binoculars to seek out birds, especially the great blue herons that frequent this area. Sometimes, these statuesque birds can be seen trying to stab fish with their sharp bills.

Cottonwood trees and willows shade the slow-moving Gunnison River. A bridge leads hikers across the river while benches serve as a place to simply watch and listen.

A word of caution: Because there is standing water along parts of the river, mosquitoes can be a problem in the summer. Use repellent.

Scrambling across a bridge on the Neversink Trail

Great Sand Dunes National Monument

What kid—or kid at heart—does not enjoy playing in a sand pile? The 39 square miles of dunes at Great Sand Dunes National Monument, located 38 highway miles northeast of Alamosa, certainly qualify. With some series of dunes rising to 700 feet, these are North America's tallest. Kids delight in the freedom of climbing the tall dunes then rolling down, or building a castle in the cool sand where the water from Medano Creek is absorbed as it flows out of the Sangre de Cristo Mountains. What makes this monument most unusual is that park interpreters take the fun of the dunes a step further. Through the use of a museum, guided hikes, Junior Ranger programs, and wonderful evening campfire programs, they explain the geology and natural history of the dunes. How the dunes came to be, how animals manage to survive in this barren place, and the roles of wind and water can all be discovered.

Camping at the monument is surprisingly good. The Pinyon Flats Campground is situated in the midst of a forest on the edge of the dunes and offers a bit of shade. Running water is available from April to October. Motorized vehicles are not allowed on the dunes themselves because that area is federally designated wilderness. But the Medano Pass Primitive Road in the nearby Rio Grande National Forest gives four-wheel-drive enthusiasts some interesting challenges. A concessionaire also conducts tours. To reach Great Sand Dunes National Monument, drive north on Colorado Highway 17 to Mosca and then turn east on Six Mile Lane. Or, driving south on US 285, take Colorado 112 east to the dunes. The monument can also be reached by driving north on Colorado 150 from US 160 near the town of Blanca.

A distant view of Great Sand Dunes National Monument

Sand Dune Hike

no specific length, year-round,
snow can close dunes at times

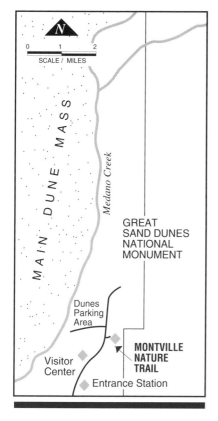

The beauty of hiking the dunes at Great Sand Dunes National Monument is that there is no trail. To parents tired of telling their children to stay on the trail in order to protect the surrounding environment, that will be welcome news. Kids will love this gigantic sand pile.

A trailhead leading to the sand dunes is at a parking and picnic area located west of the visitor center with restrooms and running water, picnic tables, and a water spigot designed to wash sand off feet.

Folks who must walk on a trail can follow previous climbers' footsteps to the top of one of the dunes. Those paths often provide clues as to the easiest way to reach the top. But it is more fun to simply turn children loose and watch what they do. All park naturalists ask is that hikers avoid the few vegetated areas that play an important role in the ecology of the monument.

Some will not get past Medano Creek. This creek flows from the nearby Sangre de Cristo Mountains, only to disappear into the dunes. In the later summer months, it may not be seen at all. The kids enjoy building sand castles, using the moist sand along the river bank as a great building material. Plan ahead by bringing sand buckets, beach balls, shovels, and Frisbees to toss around the huge expanses of sand. Some visitors go so far as to bring plastic

A solitary hiker at Great Sand Dunes National Monument

sleds to slide down the dunes. Others enjoy flying a kite. Still others will scamper up the nearest dune and then delight in jumping, tumbling, or rolling down the steep incline. This place is like spending a day at a beach without the ocean.

Early in the day, before hikers tromp all over the dunes, it is possible to see evidence of little dramas from the night before. Sets of tiny footprints can be seen crisscrossing the sand. Then, in a place where it looks as if a struggle occurred, the footprints will suddenly disappear.

Those who want to challenge the 700-foot-high dune mass may want to get up early in the morning before the sun turns the dunes into an inferno. Though it feels good to hike barefooted, wearing light tennis shoes or any enclosed footwear is a good idea. Sandals are not encouraged because the loose sand between sandal and toes can be irritating. In the middle of the day, the dunes can turn hot, making barefoot hiking a miserable experience.

When planning longer explorations of the dunes, be sure to take plenty of water. In fact, water is a good idea any season, any time of day. Having a good sunblock is also a must. The sun tends to reflect off the dunes, creating more chance for burning.

Surprisingly, hiking in the soft sand can be a difficult and challenging experience. Chances are, thigh muscles required to walk up the dunes will ache the next day.

The dunes are a photographer's paradise, especially early and late in the day, when the shadows begin to create exotic patterns and the light seems to change every few moments.

Montville Nature Trail

0.5 mile, loop, year-round,
though snow can close it at times

The trailhead of the Montville Nature Trail can be reached by car, a short stroll from the visitor center, or a 1-mile hike from the campground. Switchbacks along the nature loop reward hikers with dramatic views of the dunes in the distance, making this an especially good trail in the evening hours. When the dunes get hot in the middle of the day, hikers can head to the shade of the forested slopes of the Sangre de Cristo Mountains.

Hikers escaping the heat on the Montville Nature Trail

The trail loops up slightly, playing tag with Mosca Creek most of the way. Shaded by aspen, water-loving Douglas fir, and white fir, the trail stays cool much of the day. Be sure to pick up the trail brochure at the trailhead to learn about the mix of habitats seen along this short walk.

In addition, the trail allows glimpses of local history. Mosca Pass, a route used by explorers and pioneers, can be reached by taking a longer hike into the Sangre de Cristo Wilderness area.

Alamosa National Wildlife Refuge

A small visitor center and museum can be reached by driving 4 miles east of Alamosa on Highway 160 and 2 miles south on El Rancho Lane, part of which is gravel. The visitor center gives out free brochures and houses some small wildlife and natural history displays and a hands-on display for children. The best time to visit is in the spring and fall when thousands of migrating sandhill cranes and a few whooping cranes visit the area. Refuge managers say the peak periods for viewing the cranes occur between March 15 and October 15. Spring is the best time to view the most birds, but many types of waterfowl and shorebirds can be seen year-round. Refuge managers say winter is the best time to view eagles, hawks, and owls in the area.

Rio Grande Riparian Area Hike

2 miles, one-way, year-round

A short hiking trail leads along the dike from the visitor center and along the Rio Grande River. Though birds can be seen in the middle of the summer or winter, the best time to take this quiet, relatively easy trek is in the early morning or late evening, right before sunset. Take plenty of insect repellent—mosquitoes can be a problem.

As with most birding expeditions, a pair of binoculars is a must. Get children to walk as quietly as possible so they can sneak up without being detected. The flat, graveled trail does not appear to get much use in the summer months, making it ideal for a quiet walk. Since it is not a loop, families can turn back any time they get tired of the scenery.

Durango–Silverton

It is early morning in Durango and, suddenly, a coal-fired steam train begins chugging along narrow-gauge tracks belching black and white smoke. The train's loud whistle echoes off the walls of old hotels as it chugs through town on its daily 45-mile trip through the San Juan Mountains into the old mining town of Silverton. There, while the train engineers prepare for the trip back to Durango, families can walk through Silverton, sampling its definitive mining-town flair.

Travelers come from all over the world to ride on the 1880s vintage train that once hauled valuable ore out of the San Juan Mountains. Children who have never ridden any train, much less one that takes a route as scenic as this one, will enjoy this relaxing excursion. The Durango & Silverton train runs from late April through the end of October. A winter holiday train runs from late November through New Year's Day. Because of its popularity, advance reservations are strongly suggested. For information, write to Durango & Silverton Narrow Gauge R.R. Co., 479 Main Avenue, Durango, Colorado 81301.

While the train is the big draw, it certainly is not the only family activity available in Durango. There are a number of good hiking trails in the forests that surround town. The town itself features an Old West atmosphere, offering a number of shopping and dining possibilities. Check out the Stratler Hotel dining room for an ambiance that feels like something out of the old television western "Gunsmoke." Most kids like visiting a fish hatchery, and there is a good one right in town. The Durango Fish Hatchery, Visitors Center, and Wildlife Museum, first opened in 1893, offers families a chance to see large fish, feed the trout, and discover how trout are raised. Horseback riding in the nearby mountains is also a popular family activity. A number of commercial outfitters rent horses and guides. Trimble Hot Springs 6 miles north of town—a national historic site—provides opportunities for swimming and soaking. Children especially enjoy the Purgatory Ski Area 25 miles north of Durango. The area is home to skiing in the winter, and in the summer the lifts are used to haul mountain

A Durango & Silverton Railroad steam engine chugging through a gorge

bikers up the hill. The Alpine Slide, where riders zoom down the mountain on a small sled over a slick track after using the lift to ride up the hill, is especially popular with children.

At Silverton, a number of short hikes or four-wheel-drive experiences are available around town. By either driving from Durango or taking the train, families can experience the atmosphere of an old mining town in a scenic mountain setting. The lure of Silverton is its many interesting shops and restaurants. Children will find stores that interest them.

Cement Creek

0.25 mile, one-way, spring–fall

Families who drive to Silverton, rather than taking the narrow gauge railroad from Durango, may need a break since the drive on a narrow highway through the splendor of southern Colorado's high peaks, though beautiful, takes great concentration. The short Cement Creek Trail and park are ideal, especially for younger children.

Memorial Park is located on the northwest corner of town at the top of Main and Greene streets. A rock-covered gravel path snakes around its restrooms, play areas, picnic tables, and tennis courts. It is perhaps 0.25 mile from start to finish and crosses two wooden bridges. It borders Cement Creek, providing open space.

This is a good place to stop for a picnic, allow the children to release some energy on the playground equipment, and take a short walk, all the while enjoying views of the scenic old mining town of Silverton.

Spud Lake

2 miles, round-trip, spring–fall

This hike wanders uphill through a shaded forest. Meandering past several beaver ponds, the trail eventually reaches the shores of a pretty alpine lake.

The trailhead is reached by driving 29 miles north of Durango on US 550 to Lime Creek Road (FS 591). Look for this turnoff at the curves just past Cascade Village. The road goes past a horseback riding concession and continues 3 miles on a dirt road up to a large beaver pond. There are several parking spaces along the road leading up to the trail. Parking space is limited, and the trail is often quite crowded. Look for the sign that says "Trail" to begin the hike. There are a few places where the trail levels off or has a short downhill grade but, most of the way, it goes uphill past wildflowers and aspen glades.

Some of the beaver ponds contain beaver lodges. Lucky hikers can occasionally watch beaver swimming in the midst of these ponds.

Spud Lake, an alpine lake, lies at the end of this captivating trail. Some families with Colorado fishing licenses will want to try their luck fishing. Others may engage in that ever-popular children's activity—skipping rocks across the surface of the lake.

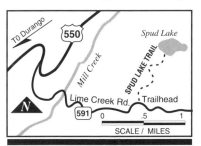

Because of the popularity of the hike, parking at the trailhead can be a problem. Families may have to park in a wide spot in the road and walk a bit farther if the lot at the trailhead is full.

Young girls enjoying quiet Spud Lake

Animas Overlook Trail

0.66 mile, loop, spring–fall

The most difficult part about taking this short and scenic 0.66-mile nature trail is getting to it. The trail is paved. Plenty of benches are located at every interpretive sign. But the winding, narrow road to the trailhead is a somewhat rough gravel and dirt road that climbs off the valley floor to the trail that overlooks the Animas River Valley below.

To reach the trailhead, turn west of Durango's Main Street on 25th Street. This street turns into Junction Street. Junction Street runs into Colorado 204. The pavement ends at the U.S. Forest Service boundary. Follow the mileposts up the mountain— passing a developed U.S. Forest Service campground along the way—to Milepost 7. Here, a large paved parking lot marks the trailhead on the right.

The signs along this gently sloping trail, first down, then up, are general to the plants and wildlife that inhabit the entire region. Some, however, contain information specific to this location. As

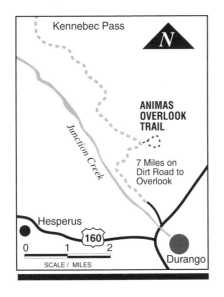

the trail winds along three sides of the mountain, the signs identify surrounding mountains and valleys. Geologic interpretations are given to explain that most of the surrounding mountains are volcanic in nature and subsequently carved by glacial action and other erosional forces.

Falls Creek, below an overlook, is the site of one of the largest concentrations of Basketmaker Indian sites in the region. Another marker explains a burned area as the result of the Forest Service's program of using controlled fires to manage the watershed that supplies 80 percent of the Animas Valley's water.

The trail is handicapped accessible with clean restrooms.

Big Al

0.75 mile, one-way, spring–fall

A less-traveled alternative to staying in Mesa Verde or a good camping choice between Durango and Cortez, the Transfer Campground area of the San Juan National Forest offers a first-rate camping experience as well as a number of short and long hiking trails. The shortest of these trails, Big Al, is handicapped accessible.

To reach the trailhead and Transfer Campground and picnic area, take US 160 through Mancos. In Mancos, take Colorado Highway 184 to the north. Right after this turn, select Colorado Road 42 to the right. The campground is 10 miles farther, mostly on a well-maintained gravel road. The trailhead for Big Al is just outside the picnic area. The trail sign is across the road.

This trail slopes gently downward at first, through wildflower meadows. It then winds its way through stands of aspen. Take

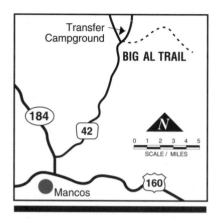

some time to find just the right size tree where an ear placed up against the trunk will hear the water gurgling in the aspen like a stream.

There are plenty of benches along the trail. This quiet spot is a good place for your children to draw, write a poem, or make up a story about the sights they have enjoyed in the Four Corners area.

The trail ends at a fenced-in balcony built out over a rock outcropping. Hikers enjoy views of the La Plata Mountains above and forest-covered hills lining Chicken Creek below.

Other longer hikes that can be enjoyed in this area include the Rim Trail, Box Canyon, and Chicken Creek.

Mesa Verde National Park

Mesa Verde means "green table" in Spanish, and for families looking for an introductory trip into the world of the Anasazi, the name is appropriate. The table is certainly set for adventure as children get a chance to explore cliff dwellings by crawling into circular kivas, discover "secret" passageways leading to incredible cliff dwellings, or use wooden ladders to climb up sandstone cliffs. Because of its popularity, the park can become crowded, especially during the summer months. For some of the more popular hikes like Balcony House and Cliff Palace, families need to get tickets at the park visitor center or museum early in the day. Because these hikes require ranger guides, they are open only during the busy tourist season (Memorial Day through Labor Day). Winter at Mesa Verde means snow, lack of crowds, and only a

A ranger introducing visitors to a Mesa Verde ruin

few open trails. Only one ruin, Spruce Tree House, is open.

The cliff dwellings that make Mesa Verde famous are extremely fragile. Expect tighter than normal controls on hiking inside the park, especially to ruins, where rangers are nearly always present. If this is the first archaeological site you visit—and it is for many families—stress to children the importance of staying on trails and keeping off fragile walls. Should a piece of pottery or other artifact be found on the trail, always leave it in place.

The park is popular, and exploring the ruins and hiking its trails is relatively easy because the trails are short, easily accessible, and well-marked. In addition, most major trails are ranger guided. There are lodge rooms, restaurants, snack bars, gas stations, laundry facilities, showers, and grocery stores inside the park. Nearby Cortez has many hotel and dining possibilities. The huge Morefield Campground, with hundreds of spaces cut out of a pinyon/juniper forest, is one of the largest in the national park system, guaranteeing a spot almost any time of year. Do not be surprised if you see mule deer roaming the campground. Remember that these are wild animals and must not be fed. Enjoy them from a distance.

Driving the 21 miles from the park entrance just south of US 160 and 10 miles from Cortez to the Chapin Mesa Museum offers families an introduction to the culture of the Anasazi before actually taking the hikes into the cliff dwellings. The Far View Visitor Center also features interpretive displays and is a place where rangers and park volunteers answer questions. Children can sign up for the park's Junior Ranger program at either the visitor center or the museum. Working to become a Junior Ranger will enhance the educational values of the trip.

Trailers and towed vehicles are prohibited beyond Morefield Campground.

Knife Edge Trail

1.5 miles, one-way, May–early October, can ski in winter

Another name for this surprisingly interesting trail might be Hummingbird Highway. This easy, gently uphill climb along the north rim of Mesa Verde near the old entrance road is lined with the wildflower called Indian paintbrush. Hummingbirds dart in and around the flowers, sampling those close to the trail. Listen and watch for them along the way. The trailhead for the Knife Edge Trail is on the western edge of Apache Loop in the Morefield Campground.

At Chapin Mesa visitors are sometimes required to climb ladders.

This trail is a great morning and an especially good evening hike because of its open exposure. It follows the original road into Mesa Verde. Gambel oaks and brushy plants can be seen along the way.

The trail brochure available at the trailhead is a wonderful plant identification guide, complete with illustrations, and a good souvenir to purchase and take home. For those who keep journals, the guide makes a good reference. It also contains interesting ethnobotany. For example, hummingbirds are not the only

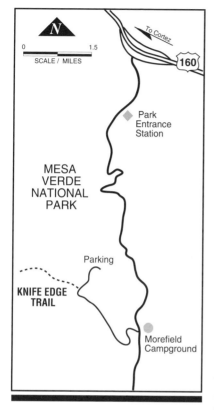

creatures who find the nectar pockets of Indian paintbrush desirable. Ute Indians chew the flowers as candy.

In addition to the hummingbirds, a number of different birds of prey and songbirds use this area. They are so plentiful that packing along a good bird identification book will help develop a family's avian identification skills.

Knife Edge Trail ends around the mesa on the west with a panoramic view of Montezuma Valley and Sleeping Ute Mountain in the distance. The unstable condition of the rocks on the rest of the trail necessitates that hikers must return back along the same trail. But, considering the number of plants and birds that might have been missed on the walk out, that is not an unpleasant task.

Chapin Mesa. For families who visit Mesa Verde to see the cliff dwellings of the ancient people who inhabited this area, Chapin Mesa is the most popular and accessible. The park's museum, with its collection of artifacts, is located here. The drive around Chapin Mesa road affords many opportunities at overlooks.

Hiking through the cliff dwellings—especially exciting treks up and down ladders and through narrow passageways found on the two guided hikes, Cliff Palace and Balcony House—makes for the most memorable experience. Tickets are required for the ranger-guided Cliff Palace and Balcony House trails during the busy summer months. They are closed to visitation during the off-season. Check at the entrance station first. Families are limited to taking one of those trails a day. A ticket can be picked up at the Far View Visitor Center and should be obtained as early in the day as possible. Rangers also request that hikers taking the longer Petroglyph Point Trail first register at the Chapin Mesa Ranger Station.

Following are descriptions of some of the main hikes on Chapin Mesa.

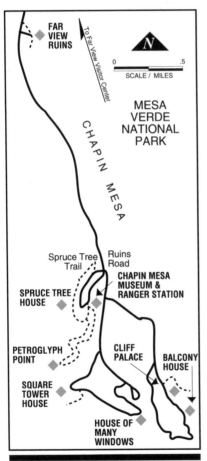

Spruce Tree House

0.75 mile, round-trip,
year-round

This is the most popular—and one of the easiest—hikes to enjoy in Mesa Verde and is the only cliff dwelling open for tours year-round. The trail is paved, so there are few surprises, but it is steep in a few spots, so expect to carry smaller youngsters.

Pick up a brochure for this self-guided trail at the trailhead by the museum and Chapin Mesa. Numbered posts correspond to explanations in the booklet. In the summer, rangers patrol the dwelling itself and are more than happy to answer questions from curious travelers.

The short trail makes a steady descent along switchbacks. At the bottom, hikers see a spring that supplied water for the 100 or so people who lived in this dwelling, the third largest in the park. Most ancient people who lived in Mesa Verde were not lucky enough to

A Mesa Verde cliff dwelling

enjoy such a steady source of water. Residents of nearby Cliff Palace, for example, had to walk over a mile for water.

The trail leads to a large cliff dwelling built under a huge red rock alcove. Kids especially enjoy crawling down the ladder into the darkness of a reconstructed circular kiva—a ceremonial structure.

During a summer evening hike, watch for the dozens of large turkey vultures that gather in the trees and on the cliffs near

Spruce Tree House. Bird lovers can watch for hours as these huge birds soar overhead or roost in nearby trees.

Petroglyph Point

2.8 miles, loop, April–October

This trail takes off from the Spruce Tree House Trail and leads to the largest and best-known petroglyph panels at Mesa Verde. Petroglyphs—the rock writings of ancient people—are not common at Mesa Verde. Larger collections of petroglyphs can be found elsewhere in the Southwest.

This is a good trail on which to escape the crowds that flock to Mesa Verde in the summer. Tour Spruce Tree House first and then, as the trail starts back up to the museum, both this trail and the Spruce Canyon Trail take off to the left and right, respectively. Before taking either of these trails, hikers need to register at the ranger station near the museum. They can also pick up a helpful trail guide while registering. The guide goes into great detail about the plants and animals of Mesa Verde as well as the ancient people who once utilized them. The guide also gives information on Mesa Verde geology, especially in this particular canyon.

The first half of the trail is fun for kids. It winds along on roughly the same level through sandstone nooks and crannies and giant, almost cliff dwelling-size, alcoves. Stairs, sometimes only kid-wide, are carved from the stone. After stop No. 7, a gigantic boulder perches over a crack that is the trail. It reminds a hiker of an Indiana Jones movie.

Another fun aspect of this trail is that every archaeological point of interest is not spelled out or revealed to hikers. Take the opportunity to use what information has been given elsewhere as clues. Then search canyon walls and alcoves with eyes or binoculars, looking for other dwellings or rock writing.

Be watchful, too, after the petroglyph panel, for the steps and hand holds that take off sharply to the left and up to the mesa top. The National Park Service requests that hikers make the whole loop and do not double back because the narrowness of the trail makes two-way traffic difficult. The last half of the trail after the petroglyph panel, however, goes directly up to the mesa top and is a flat walk through the pinyon/juniper forest.

Near the visitor center, hikers get an opportunity for a different view of Spruce Tree House from the head of the canyon.

Balcony House

0.5 mile, round-trip, mid-May–mid-September

A guided tour through Balcony House is guaranteed to stretch a child's imagination. Even MTV-jaded teenagers get excited climbing the ladders and crawling through the narrow passageways of this relatively short but exciting trail that takes just under an hour to complete. Remember that tickets, which assign a specific time to a family, are required on this hike.

While waiting in line at the top of the trailhead, parents might ask their children a few questions. Why would ancient people build a cliff dwelling under a hard-to-reach alcove? How would they haul food and water into such a place, or dispose of their garbage? What would life for a child be like in a place like this?

Cliff dwelling at Mesa Verde

A ranger greets visitors and directs them to a small area near the paved trail. The trail almost seems to lead into oblivion but is carved along the edge of a sandstone cliff. Each ranger brings his or her personality to the guided hike, offering insights, answering questions, and often telling humorous stories.

The incredible Balcony House cliff dwelling is built under an alcove. The ranger stops to explain different aspects of Puebloan life. Then the fun begins. In order to move from one part of the cliff dwelling to another, hikers must crawl on their hands and knees through a dark, narrow passageway. That accomplished, they then climb a tall ladder straight up and out to the parking lot. This makes the hike inappropriate for extremely young children or adults with a fear of heights or tight spaces. For most, it simply makes this hike one of the Southwest's most exciting family adventures.

Cliff Palace

0.75 mile, round-trip, mid-April–mid-October,
road closed to vehicles in winter but open for skiing

Like Balcony House, Cliff Palace also combines the thrill of climbing ladders and the information provided by a ranger-guided hike. The climb is easier than others, making this a more appropriate adventure for younger children or adults who do not want to crawl on their hands and knees. The trailhead is on the north side of the ruins road. Plan on spending just under an hour completing the tour.

The four-story Cliff Palace, built under an alcove that is 324 feet long, 89 feet deep, and 59 feet high, is the largest of the park's many impressive cliff dwellings. It is a place that truly displays the remarkable architectural and aesthetic genius of the ancient people who lived here.

Remember that advance tickets are required for this hike and a time is assigned to each group. The ranger greets hikers at the trailhead and escorts them on a short walk through a pinyon/juniper forest on a paved trail that eventually winds down the side of the sandstone cliff. Chances are the ranger will stop on the trail to allow photographers a chance to snap pictures of the entire cliff dwelling from some strategic overlook.

Each guided tour is different. Some rangers like to emphasize Puebloan life. Others concentrate on how the dwellings were constructed. Some go into how Anglos discovered Cliff Palace, how it was reconstructed, stabilized, and preserved, and what lessons modern people can learn from the Ancient Ones. Encourage children to ask the ranger questions or offer their own theories as they get a chance to tour the ruin complex, learning about the ancient inhabitants who built these cliff dwellings.

Wetherill Mesa. Named after Richard Wetherill, the cowboy from nearby Mancos who is credited with discovering the cliff dwellings in 1888, this is the less visited part of Mesa Verde National Park. Accessible only in the summer by driving a narrow paved

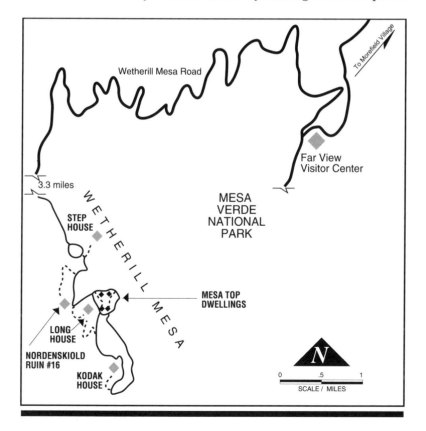

A family exploring Long House Ruin

but twisting 12-mile road from Far View, the hiking trails in this part of the park are generally less crowded than those on Chapin Mesa. Vehicles weighing over 8,000 pounds or over 25 feet in length are not allowed on the road. Free trams (small train-like motorized vehicles) run on a regular basis and take visitors to trailheads or overlooks from where they can hike or take photos. Badger House, located on the mesa top and not a cliff dwelling, also makes for a fine hike. The advantage of the tram system is that families can take long or short hikes. When young legs get tired, a tram ride is not far away. Families can ride the tram to see Kodak House and Nordenskiold Ruin. Most of the hikes into the cliff dwellings involve hiking with a ranger. Sign up for some of the special guided hikes as well. There is a small snack bar and picnic area near the parking area.

Long House Ruin

1 mile, round-trip, Memorial Day–Labor Day

This ranger-guided hike starts at the Ranger Contact Station at Wetherill Mesa and involves a short downhill walk on a paved trail that leads to the longest alcove in the park. Because it is tucked back so far under the alcove, 90 percent of the dwelling is in its original condition, a feature that makes it unique. Only a few walls have been stabilized in the front area to protect them from visitors.

The dwelling also features an open work area and spring in the back of the alcove, both of which can be accessed by visitors using ten- and fifteen-rung ladders. Here, in the shade of the alcove, families can actually feel how cool it would be to work in this cliff dwelling, even on the hottest summer day. The spring provides a sort of natural air conditioning. Grooves where people ground corn remain in the soft sandstone floor. One kiva—a ceremonial room— has a reconstructed roof covered with a metal grating.

Badger House Ruin

0.75 mile, one-way, Memorial Day–Labor Day

The Badger House Community Trail starts at the Ranger Contact Station at Wetherill Mesa and is mostly level or down-hill. Hikers are picked up on each end by the tram. The trail leads through the pinyon/juniper forest of the mesa top and leads to four sites, each covered by a pavilion and fenced in so visitors cannot walk near the fragile ruins. At any of these four stops, a short trail leads back to the tram pick-up point.

This trail is important because it fills in the historic picture of ancient peoples in the Southwest. While the ancient tribes began living in caves, they eventually constructed pithouses on the mesa tops before building the cliff dwellings. An excavation of such a pithouse is found at the first stop. Interpretive signs at the site and throughout the park place this and other dwellings on a timeline of Puebloan history. After the pithouses—at about A.D. 750—the picture began to change and rooms were built above ground. Hikers can view an excavated Pueblo village with a great kiva, one large enough to service a larger surrounding population.

Badger House contains a tower connected by a 41-foot tunnel to a kiva. Archaeologists are unsure of the significance of this tower. Visitors develop their own theories.

The final dwelling site, Two Raven House, was a Pueblo site with some unusual functions. It has a stone pit built apart from the dwelling that could have been an oven. It has posts arranged around the plaza of the pueblo that could have supported a fence whose purpose is unclear. Perhaps it was a windbreak or maybe it was used to keep animals in or out. Maybe all pueblos had such a structure, but archaeologists have yet to discover them.

The trail to Step House Ruin is also accessible from the parking area. This is unusual in that sites from the Basketmaker and Pueblo eras are found together.

Nordenskiold Ruin

1.5 miles, round-trip, Memorial Day–Labor Day

At the Wetherill Mesa Ranger Contact Station near the parking area, ask a ranger to point out the wood-chip path to Nordenskiold Ruin. This trail is also accessible from the tram loop road. Hikers can ask to be dropped off at the trailhead.

This trail leads to an overlook of Ruin #16 and traverses a mostly flat pinyon/juniper forest. The trail guide available at the trailhead includes valuable information on the plants of this forest. Look for the access route the ancient inhabitants used somewhere along the rock shelf on the same level as the dwellings. Those who look closely can usually find a crack or crevice where steps or toe holds can be discovered.

The trail dips down at the end to overlook the ruins. This is a site that was inhabited by perhaps twenty or thirty people. Like most dwellings in Mesa Verde, it is far from the bottom of the canyon up a steep wall. It is an alcove with solid rock above it.

Anasazi Heritage Center

Located on Colorado Highway 184, 3 miles northwest of Dolores on the banks of McPhee Reservoir, this modern Bureau of Land Management-operated museum utilizes a variety of hands-on activities to introduce visitors to the ancient people who once inhabited this area. Children can try weaving on a loom like those traditional Navajos use on the nearby reservation. They can grind corn on an ancient mano and metate. They can touch artifacts usually found locked behind glass doors at other museums. Several drawers contain artifacts, including pieces of pottery, stone axes, and bone tools. Microscopes are available to allow examination of ancient artifacts as small as pollen. Another exhibit offers a look at a reconstructed pithouse similar to those found in the area. Visitors examine the re-created cross-section of ground at a dig that shows what archaeologists must sift through to find artifacts. Another exhibit shows how scientists use artifacts found at ruin sites to reach conclusions about a particular period of human history. Before McPhee Reservoir flooded some of the surrounding area, archaeologists collected as many artifacts as possible. Most are stored at the museum. "Behind the Scenes" tours of these collections are often available. Computer games in the museum quiz visitors on what they learned in the museum tour. A video on the development of the museum, construction of the reservoir, and history of the ancient people is also available at the visitor center.

Dominguez and Escalante Ruins Hike

1 mile, round-trip, year-round

Located just outside the Anasazi Heritage Center, the Dominguez ruins can be viewed by simply taking a short walk west of the parking area. A 0.5-mile-long paved trail—which is handicapped accessible and suitable for baby strollers—leads to the

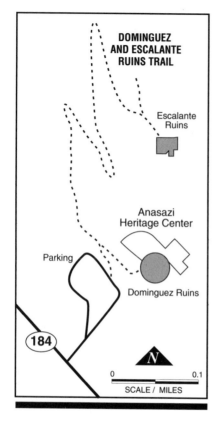

Escalante Ruin as well as a viewpoint overlooking McPhee Reservoir, which furnishes water to the surrounding area. A self-guiding trail brochure is available at the trailhead. It describes the ancient inhabitants of this area in general and those who lived in this small village in detail.

Spanish priests Francisco Anastasio Dominguez and Silvestre Velez de Escalante, spotted the ruins during their journey from Santa Fe to an area just south of what is now Salt Lake City in 1776 and 1777. Archaeologists have partially excavated the Escalante ruins. Low walls and a kiva can be viewed on the site. The ruins are thought to have been part of an extensive trade and cultural system centered in Chaco Canyon to the south. Masonry and pottery styles here and at the larger Chaco site are similar.

New Mexico

It is festival day at the Santa Clara Pueblo north of Santa Fe, and an eclectic blend of cultures gathers at the main square. While colorfully dressed Native Americans perform a traditional corn dance, a German tourist purchases an African-made basket from a Hispanic woman.

Such is the kaleidoscope of cultures that make up New Mexico. Families looking primarily for outdoor experiences can learn much from a visit to this land of towering alpine mountain peaks and desolate red deserts. One of the purposes of family travel, whether on a weekend excursion or a trip around the world, should be to expand the knowledge of adult and child. In this regard, New Mexico delivers.

Wander through the ancient plazas of Santa Fe, Taos, or Albuquerque, where Indian, Mexican, and American history forged the culture that makes this land so different from most other places in the United States. Shop for Acoma, Santa Clara, or San

Ildefonso pottery, Navajo jewelry, or Hispanic artwork. Enjoy the mix of foods, music, legend, and history. On a single day, climb up a steep ladder into an ancient Anasazi ruin at Bandelier National Monument in the morning and, later that afternoon, discover the history of the atomic bomb at a museum in nearby Los Alamos.

While visiting major northern New Mexico cities such as Santa Fe, Gallup, Albuquerque, and Taos, enjoy different types of outdoor hiking experiences. In the morning, walk along a nature trail in a lush national forest. During the hot part of the day, visit an air-conditioned museum in town after sampling the local cuisine at lunch. Later, wander through a desert monument where the churches of ancient peoples sit next to those of Spanish priests. Climb a ladder down into a kiva, the ceremonial chamber of the Anasazi, and sit with your children in dark silence, contemplating the spirituality of a culture that flourished during Europe's Dark Ages.

The goals of a good family vacation should be to educate and entertain. The historical cities of Taos, Santa Fe, and Albuquerque—and the rugged land that surrounds them—serve as places to achieve those goals for both parents and children.

Taos

Taos, located in north central New Mexico with the high peaks of the Carson National Forest as a backdrop, returns families to the past. Though hunter-gatherers lived here as far back as 9000 B.C., prehistoric ruins dating from A.D. 900 to A.D. 1300 hint at a sophisticated culture. The ancient people who lived here left no written record, forcing modern archaeologists to use the clues left behind in an attempt to solve many puzzles about the lives and culture of the Anasazi. Hints about what life was like in the ancient ruins can be found by visiting the modern-day Taos Pueblo north of town. This pueblo, still inhabited by people whose ancestors predate the Spanish, links the past with the present.

The first Spaniards arrived in Taos Valley in 1540. A Spanish officer, scouting for the Coronado expedition, is credited with being the first to explore the area, but the Spaniards did not colonize it until 1598. Taos Pueblo inhabitants drove the Spaniards and their priests out of the province in 1680 and again in 1696, after repeated colonization attempts. In the mid-1700s, Plains Indian raids made life difficult for the settlers. In the early 1800s, the town became headquarters for famous mountain men such as Kit Carson, who made his home in Taos from 1826 to 1868. This residence, near the town's historic plaza, is now a state park and a museum. Families can also see what living during this time was like by visiting the Martinez Hacienda, which illustrates the life of a Spanish colonial family.

In the late 1800s, artists discovered Taos. Painting vistas of the surrounding mountains and deserts as well as its unique people, the artists turned Taos into a well-known cultural mecca. Families who enjoy art like to visit the Millicent Rogers Museum, Harwood Foundation Museum, Blumenschein Home and Museum, or Fechin Institute. Simply taking a stroll through the historic plaza, with its many dazzling shops, can be enjoyable for families searching for souvenirs or original works of art.

Families also enjoy taking a break from hiking by taking a ride

A historic church at Taos

on the Cumbres and Toltec Scenic Railroad. Drive 60 miles south from Taos to Antonito, Colorado, and ride the steam locomotive over 10,015-foot Cumbres Pass and 1,100-foot-deep Toltec Gorge to the town of Chama.

In modern times, the building of nearby ski areas such as Taos Ski Valley, Angel Fire, Red River, Ski Rio, or Sipapu helped turn Taos into a winter and summer destination resort, offering visitors plenty of tourist facilities for skiing, mountain biking, and hiking.

Write to the Taos County Chamber of Commerce (see Appendix) and specifically request "The Kid's Guide to Taos," which is full of ideas for family travel.

Carson National Forest

The Carson National Forest surrounds Taos. Though many of the hikes in the area might be longer than families with young children want to tackle, a few outfitters are available to take adventurers into nearby wilderness areas. There are several good and fairly easy day hikes within an hour's drive of town that families can enjoy. Stop at the Carson National Forest office or Chamber of Commerce office in Taos to obtain information.

Cebolla Mesa Trail

2 miles, one-way, spring–fall

The trailhead for this moderately difficult hike to the confluence of the Red and Rio Grande rivers is located 19 miles north of Taos. Take Highway 522 out of town. Look for a faded U.S. Forest Service sign marking Forest Road 9. This slightly rutted dirt road travels west 3 miles to Cebolla Mesa and an undeveloped campground that overlooks the Rio Grande River. Toward the start of the drive on Forest Road 9, the road forks. Take the left fork that, at one point, follows a powerline.

Cebolla Mesa Trail leads hikers down to the Rio Grande River.

The trailhead to this portion of the U.S. Wild and Scenic River system begins near a sign in the parking area. Primitive restrooms—but no water—are available. Since the hike involves a steep climb into the gorge, bring plenty of liquid refreshment. Near its start, the well-marked trail soon branches into three trails. Take the one to the left, which is the most well defined. Then begin the steady and, at times, steep descent into the river gorge. Four long switchbacks lead through a pinyon/juniper forest, offering views of the blue-green water of the Rio Grande River below. About halfway down, the trail traverses a bench. The final portion of the trail leads through a ponderosa forest. Since the canyon is steeply cut from dark, volcanic basalt, hikers marvel at the places where angular, jagged boulders have been smoothed, shined, and sculpted by the river.

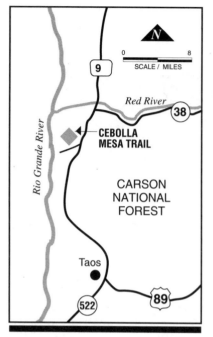

At the bottom, the smaller Red River joins with the Rio Grande, creating a lush band of green guaranteed to delight children. A bridge on the trail leads over the Red River to two covered picnic areas and a pit toilet. Families who enjoy fishing like to try their luck for trout in the waters of the Rio Grande. Most, though, enjoy simply skipping rocks or relaxing and enjoying the solitude. The river can be swift and deep, so children should be watched closely.

The climb leads back up the same route. Though moderately steep, children as young as five or six should have no trouble completing the trek. There are plenty of nice, large rocks under shade trees where families can take a break.

Agua Piedra Nature Trail

0.8 mile, loop, May–late November

Families looking for more of an alpine experience and an introduction to the Sangre de Cristo Mountains south and east of Taos can make the half-hour drive from Taos on Highway 518 into the Rio Pueblo area of the Camino Real Ranger District of the Carson National Forest. There they will find a handicapped-accessible 0.8-mile loop called the Agua Piedra Nature Trail. This inviting children's trail is located off Highway 518 with a sign and a parking area just south of a developed U.S. Forest Service campground by the same name. In a region of New Mexico where good public campgrounds can be difficult to find, those along Highway 518 rank with the best.

Though most hikes in the range are well over 3 miles, this one

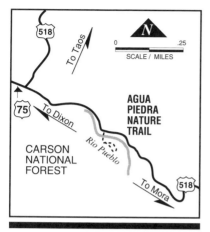

is short, flat, and easy. Because stream rehabilitation work has created several nice fishing holes and because handicapped-accessible fishing piers reach over into the stream, this is also an ideal place to introduce children to the joys of trout fishing.

The trail parallels the Rio Pueblo, a pretty stream that flows through the canyon. Signs along the route invite hikers to stop, listen, observe, and learn about this river ecosystem. Since only two percent of the land in New Mexico consists of the valuable green spaces on either side of a flowing stream, those who take the hike quickly learn how important a place like this is to wild creatures and plants.

Open, grassy meadows filled with wild daisies and asters greet hikers. A sign calls these places "nature's grocery store" because of their value to elk, deer, and other animals children might see along the way. Encourage children to sit quietly on one of the benches and simply observe. Chances are they will see wildlife that will make the trip here more memorable.

The trail ends at a filled-in beaver pond. Look for the stumps that bear the beaver's characteristic gnawing both here and on the return trip around the loop.

A child studying an interpretive sign on the Aqua Piedra Nature Trail

Santa Fe–Los Alamos

Though located only 34 road miles apart, the historical differences between the old Spanish town of Santa Fe and the bustling modern government enclave of Los Alamos are great, but the two cities share some similarities: They are close to good skiing, interesting cultural history, and some fine outdoor experiences.

Santa Fe celebrates its colorful past with some of the oldest European-style squares and buildings found in the United States. After all, the city dates back to 1598 and has been the capital city of either the province of Nuevo Mexico or the State of New Mexico since 1610. Careful planning and zoning, which limit the height of buildings and impart a definite Southwestern flair to the architecture, make wandering through the art shops, restaurants, churches, and museums of Santa Fe one of America's most delightful experiences. Though older children may enjoy shopping and wandering through art galleries, youngsters can get bored quickly. But they should enjoy visiting the Museum of International Folk Art. Young children love the brightly decorated toys in the main hall, set up in dioramas depicting scenes from around the world. They should also like the Santa Fe Children's Museum or El Rancho de las Golondrinas, a 200-acre living history area where visitors learn about the lifestyle of the earliest settlers to this area. The Palace of the Governors, the oldest public building in the United States, located on Santa Fe's main square, also gives families an interesting historical tour. Older children often enjoy purchasing inexpensive items from Native American artists who sell their wares under the Palace's long covered portal. In the winter, skiers take to the slopes at the Santa Fe Ski Area.

When driving between Santa Fe and Los Alamos on US 84–285, families may want to visit a Native American pueblo such as Santa Clara or San Ildefonso. This will require a stop at pueblo headquarters to gain permission or, at times, payment of a small fee. Some of the pueblos are closed to the public, except on special feast days. Check calendars or inquire at visitor centers for those dates. A few of the larger pueblos also feature museums.

Los Alamos sprang to life as a secret community in 1941 when some of the world's most brilliant scientists gathered for the Manhattan Project, the building of the first atomic bomb. The free Bradbury Science Museum, located in the heart of this government town, is a "don't miss" attraction for families. Though one wing of the museum traces the history of the Manhattan Project, other parts offer glimpses at the more peaceful uses of atomic energy now being studied at Los Alamos. Because almost all of the exhibits are of the hands-on variety, children can spend a half day pulling levers, conducting their own experiments, typing on interactive computers, or watching live demonstrations.

In the winter, the Pajarito Ski Area offers inexpensive skiing on the edge of town.

Puye Cliff Dwellings

0.5 mile, round-trip, year-round

Families can spend 20 minutes or 2 hours exploring these cliff dwellings on the Santa Clara Indian Reservation. Though the entrance fee is slightly more expensive than comparable state and national park facilities, most find exploring these ruins worth the extra charge.

When paying the fee, visitors are given a walking brochure. The trail leads up from a small visitor center with eight ruin sites marked. Families with a sense of adventure can climb up ancient stairs and wooden ladders—one with twenty-one rungs—to reach the mesa top. Some steep stairways—really just stepping places carved out of the volcanic tuff—also lead to the top. Those with younger children may want to drive their car to the top of the mesa.

Trails lead out along the steep cliff edge to two levels of ruins. The caves that served as the rear area of the cliff dwellings are plentiful. The doorways—which are child-size—lead into some interesting rooms. On blistering hot summer days, visitors will find these back rooms surprisingly cool and quiet. Plaster and soot from ancient fires can be viewed in many of these rooms. Look for rock writing on the walls of the cliff.

Though there are trail markers, the hike leads off in several directions, making for more adventure. At marker 7, explorers can enter a kiva—the circular underground chamber where ancient people performed religious ceremonies. There is another kiva on the upper level of the cliff dwellings perched at the end of the trail.

At the mesa top, hikers discover a large ruin complex and additional pueblos. At marker 8, a ruin called the Community House features walls made of volcanic tuff.

While it is exciting to literally walk in the same footpaths as the Ancient Ones, parents need to watch their children closely at this site. Footing can be slippery where the tuff steps have filled with sand. Many of the trails lead to the edge of steep cliffs. Make certain children stay off walls of ancient ruins.

Bandelier National Monument

Each Four Corners national park, monument, or historic area celebrating the history of the ancient people who inhabited the area hundreds of years ago has its own personality. At Bandelier, 46 miles west of Santa Fe, some of the dwellings have been carved out of tuff, a soft rock formed of consolidated hot ash from a nearby volcano. In addition to more traditional dwellings built on the canyon floor, the rooms cut out of the canyon walls provide children with interesting places to explore. From Santa Fe, monument headquarters can be reached by driving north on US 285 to Pojoaque, then west on New Mexico 502 and south on New Mexico 4. From May through September, the number of people visiting monument headquarters and Frijoles Canyon can overwhelm facilities. There are times when there are more cars than parking spaces, and often there is a wait for parking at midday. Because of this, parking in the main lot is restricted to vehicles 17 feet and under. Vehicles longer than that must park across the bridge in either the backcountry lot or picnic area. A good way to beat the crowds, especially when camping in the monument, is to get an early start. There is a small museum at the visitor center in Frijoles Canyon with video programs on the area's history. At times, during the summer months, native artists work on the visitor center patio, answering questions and showing their techniques. The center is also a place where children can sign up for the monument's Junior Ranger program. A gift shop and snack bar can also be found on the site. A nice, shaded picnic area is located near the visitor center.

The 94-unit Juniper Family Campground, located in a scenic juniper forest near the monument entrance, ranks among the better facilities in the Four Corners area. No reservations are taken, and the campground can fill during the busy summer months, so families should arrive early. It is closed December through February. There is a maximum of ten people, three tents, and two vehicles per site. A large amphitheater offers very worthwhile evening programs.

There is no overnight lodging, but motels are available in nearby Los Alamos, White Rock, and Santa Fe. Families seeking solitude can consider backpacking in the 32,000-acre monument. Free permits are required for overnight travel.

Frijoles Canyon Trail

1.5 miles, loop, year-round,
snow may close trail periodically in winter

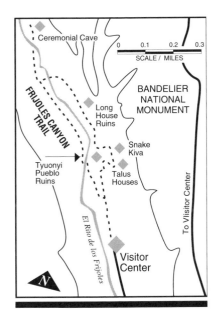

On an early morning hike just after sunrise, before the parking lot fills with visitors from all over the world, this trail can be a magical place. Colorful birds flit from tree to tree, sometimes stopping for water in the creek, El Rito de los Frijoles, which runs through the canyon.

The trail begins near the creek at the visitor center, where a self-guiding brochure is available. It leads through a large ground-level pueblo ruin and several cliff houses. The trail is either paved or developed along rock. To enter cliff

Kids peeking out of a Frijoles Canyon ruin

dwellings and a kiva, hikers must be prepared to climb ladders and stairs cut into the volcanic tuff. This makes exciting hiking for children but requires parents to be alert for potential dangers. Everyone must stay on the trail at all times with parents remaining with their children.

Hiking to Ceremonial Cave, perhaps the most exciting place to visit in the national monument, is an additional 1-mile round trip that begins at the northwest corner of the nature trail. The level walk to the base of the cave is relatively easy, but to enter the cave itself hikers must climb 140 feet up, mostly using ladders. None of these are for the faint of heart or the overprotective parent. If such adventures make parents leery, it is best not to hike to the base of the cave because most children will immediately want to begin climbing the ladders.

The nature trail begins near the creek. Informative signs describe the area's natural history and add information not found in the trail guide. Signs describing the birds and reptiles are especially helpful because those who take the time to look can see incredible numbers of birds, lizards, and small mammals along the way. Morning and evening are the best times to view wildlife.

Leaving the visitor center on the main ruins loop, the first ruins are those of Tyuonyi. This area consists of a large 400-room pueblo and would have housed about 100 people. This valley-floor pueblo was occupied at the same time as the nearby cliff dwellings, making this a bustling city 600 years ago. At marker 9, hikers can choose to climb ladders along the marked trail or take the left trail that bypasses the cliff dwellings but leads to Long House Ruins at the base of the cliffs.

If hikers stay on the nature trail, they walk up to the spongecake-like cliffs of volcanic tuff, passing cholla cactus and flowering jimson weed. At marker 11, notice how footsteps in the cave sound like drum beats. The reconstructed Talus House at marker 12 is the only dwelling with rebuilt walls. It gives visitors an idea of what the pueblos may have looked like. From here, hikers get a good overall view of the Tyuonyi ruins at the bottom of the canyon. The trail then leads to a larger cave with plaster remaining on some of its walls. At Snake Kiva at marker 13, look closely for the pictograph of a snake on the wall.

The National Park Service has built railings along the trickiest portions of the trail. At marker 15, hikers reach a cave kiva that is, at first, revealed only by a small hole in the wall. It makes a hiker wonder how many kivas are behind all the holes in the canyon walls.

The trail soon divides again. Left leads back to the visitor center. Right takes hikers past an historic orchard to Long House Ruins. Look for petroglyphs at roof level when reaching marker 20. The trail then follows the base of the cliffs, and a boardwalk takes visitors to a view of a painting on original wall plaster, protected by glass. A cave 50 feet above the trail is home to bats during the summer. Their droppings are piled up below the cave. Listen carefully for bat sounds. Though the ruins are closed at night, the Park Service often leads sunset hikes to this spot for interpretive talks on the bats. Check at the visitor center for details.

The trail then leads to El Rito de los Frijoles. Hikers can decide to finish the loop by walking on the shaded nature trail back to the visitor center or to head right to Ceremonial Cave. This trail is a beautiful stroll through a forest of tall ponderosa pine.

Hikers should train their eyes to look along the south-facing canyon walls for more dwellings. Binoculars come in handy on this hike, both for searching for rock writings and dwellings and for watching birds.

Ceremonial Cave formerly held a two-story, 22-room dwelling with a small kiva, under an alcove. The heart-stopping ascent—which includes ladders with thirteen, nineteen, and twenty-six rungs as well as stone steps cut into the cliffs—leads to the alcove. After reaching the top of the second ladder, look for a jug-handle arch in the nearby wall. Inside the cave itself, hikers can climb into a restored kiva or simply take time to stare out at the world as ancient people once did. This place gives children the feeling of a true "cliff" dwelling perched high above the canyon floor.

Taking the return nature trail to the visitor center, encourage older children to read the informative signs that contain information on the ecosystems of Bandelier, the role of fire, and the area's geology.

Falls Trail

2 miles, one-way, year-round,
snow may close trail periodically in winter

In the cool of morning, this fairly easy hike to Upper Falls with another 0.5 mile to Lower Falls seems like a pleasant walk through the woods. Though there is a 400-foot elevation gain on the way back, most children will have no trouble making the trip. Those taking the hike during the hot portion of a summer day, however,

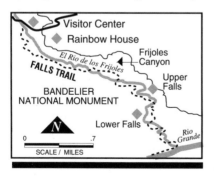

may find it more difficult. In either case, take a good supply of water.

The trailhead can be reached by driving to the Bandelier Visitor Center and then parking near the picnic area. Because this is a popular hiking trail—and parking at the monument is somewhat limited—hikers may have to walk a block or so to reach the trailhead. Just after the trail begins, it splits. Stay on the more heavily used trail.

Because the Falls Trail passes through three distinct plant communities, it provides parents a chance to teach an ecology lesson. The well-written trail guide—which can be purchased or borrowed at the visitor center—helps point out the differences. Have each family member select a favorite plant and count that plant along the way, seeing how common each plant is. Look for sagebrush and yucca in the Falls area and wherever there is little water. Narrowleaf cottonwood is found along streams. The canyon walls are home to pinyon, juniper, and ponderosa. As the trail heads up to the drier, more exposed hillsides, note how the tall ponderosa act like ladders. Their roots are near the stream, and their tops are in the dry pinyon/juniper forest. At one point after the first stream crossing, a long ponderosa lies next to the trail. Have children figure ways to measure both the diameter and height of this monster.

The trail also teaches a wonderful geology lesson. Two types of igneous—or volcanic—rock are found here. Eruptions of the nearby Jemez volcanic field covered the area with ash almost a million years ago. The tuff that resulted from those eruptions provided a place where ancient people constructed the nearby cliff dwellings. A darker, harder rock called basalt can also be seen. It is this darker rock, the result of lava flows from volcanoes to the southeast, that ancient people used to create stone tools and grinders. While hiking the first part of the trail, look for evidence of past fires, a necessary part of the forest system that helps return needed nutrients to the soil.

At marker 5, examine the twisted and pocked tuff formation. Challenge children to find other words or things that remind them of this rock. Foam rubber, bone marrow, or honeycombs come to mind.

After the second stream crossing, the trail rises and the canyon narrows through the dark basalt. The Upper Falls can be heard before they are seen.

At marker 14, take a look at the opposite wall. This clearly shows a cross-section of a volcano, cut out by El Rito de los Frijoles. This lighter sandstone-like rock was formed when water flowed into a volcanic vent, hitting magma and glass particles and throwing up steam and rock. The cone filled after many eruptions so that no water could enter and later was covered by flows of lava that cooled into harder rock.

Upper Falls cascades down such dark rock. It is off limits to hikers, who can view it from above. A cool, shady respite can be found after walking down three switchbacks toward Lower Falls. Here, the trail stops in a flat area. The trail then extends from this shady area to a rocky ledge where Lower Falls is visible. From that point, families may want to hike another 0.5 mile downhill to the edge of the Rio Grande River.

Tsankawi Ruins Trail

1.5 miles, loop,
snow may close trail periodically in winter

Looking to turn on a child's imagination and powers of observation through the use of an incredible outdoor experience? This trail, located 11 miles north of the main portion of Bandelier National Monument on New Mexico Highway 4, is guaranteed to do that and much more.

It often seems that every rock, mesa, and wall in this area holds a petroglyph, ancient cave dwelling, or ruin. Walt Disney himself could not have dreamed up the myriad of caves, cubbyholes, chutes, and ladders that ancient people carved into the

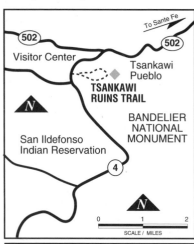

white volcanic tuff at Tsankawi. Hikers can view unexcavated ruins on the top of the mesa and dwellings on the cliffs below.

A small parking lot at the trailhead leads to a visitor contact station. Those who have not visited the main monument will need to pay an entrance fee. A trail brochure is available at the contact station, where a ranger is often on hand to answer questions. Pay close attention to warnings of steep dropoffs and narrow trails cut into the soft rock by centuries of foot traffic.

Bring along binoculars to help spot archaeological sites on this mesa and another south-facing wall to the north. To those who have visited Chaco Canyon or Hovenweep, seeing what unexcavated ruins look like can prove interesting. Look for places where the vegetation is different from surrounding areas. Also, children might be tempted to take home some of the ancient pottery sherds occasionally found on this trail. This is not only unethical but illegal as well. If a piece of pottery is found, use the opportunity to teach a lesson. First, if everyone who hiked this trail took a piece of pottery, there would not be any left for others to see. Second, sometimes the smallest piece can provide a valuable clue for

Squeezing through a narrow passage at Bandelier National Monument

archaeologists studying the area. Removing or moving evidence can damage such studies. Third, and not least, many Native Americans consider these remnants part of their heritage and wish them left where found. So, while it is enjoyable to find and look at ancient pottery sherds found along the trail, urge children to look at them and put them back. They serve as touchstones reminding modern hikers of the commonality they share with ancient people. They remind today's explorers that the basics—a place to live, something to eat, and a desire for beauty—have been passed down through the ages.

At the top of the mesa, near marker 10, hikers reach Tsankawi Pueblo, a two- to three-story village built sometime in the 1400s after the ancient people moved from smaller pueblos and cliff dwellings. It contains about 350 rooms.

Soon afterward, the trail descends a 12-foot ladder from the cliff edge down to more dwellings. To the west, an unnumbered trail leads around the mesa on a somewhat precarious trail. Hikers can view petroglyphs and ruins. The majority of the cliff dwellings, though, can be found on the marked trail to the right where trails lead to small caves and a honeycomb of tunnels, stairs, and passageways. Stop and listen to the sounds in a cave and feel the spirits of the ancient people who lived here. In some caves, hikers will find rock writing, plaster, or soot from ancient fires.

The trail back to the parking area is an old path worn deep into the soft rock. There are times when a hiker feels like a marble in a chute. Because the trail parallels the cliff in places, with a sheer drop along the side, go slowly, all the while looking for evidence of ancient people.

Pecos National Monument

A modern visitor center, complete with computer education programs and an active Junior Ranger program, make this park well worth the drive off Interstate 25, 25 miles south of Santa Fe.

Interpretive displays are in English and Spanish, a reflection that this area was once a part of Mexico. Greer Garson's husband, "Buddy," donated some of the park's land and the visitor center. Ms. Garson narrates the film that is shown regularly at the visitor center.

Pecos Trail to Pueblo and Mission

1.25 miles, loop, year-round

This easy-to-walk paved trail documents a critical link in the chronology of the Southwest. Using information from the visitor center, the trail guide, and signs along the way, hikers can make the link between ancient Native American cultures and the coming of the Spaniards.

Pecos, built over an earlier site, thrived as an active pueblo in the 1400s. Located on a trade route, Plains tribes—usually Apaches—met and exchanged slaves, buffalo skins, flint, and shells for the Pueblo's crops, turquoise, and cloth. Pecos Pueblo also turned out to be on the route taken by Spanish conquistador Francisco Vasquez de Coronado on his expedition north looking for the famed Seven Cities of Gold. That led to the site becoming a Spanish mission. It was also close to a Civil War battle. Of major significance, too, is the fact that the Pueblo of Pecos exists today at the Pueblo of Jemez, tying ancient tribes with more modern Native Americans. Thus, for families using their Southwest travels as a way to give their children a feel for history, taking this hike helps link many of the area's most significant events.

As the trail begins, look to a large mound covered with grass.

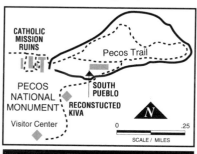

That is what remains of a huge pueblo that once was four stories high in places and served as home for 2,000 inhabitants. Tens of thousands of bushels of corn were once stored here.

Adding to a child's interest is the fact that, early in the trail, a reconstructed kiva invites visitors to climb down a

The remains of a mission at Pecos National Monument

ladder into a darkened circular underground chamber. At the touch of a button, recorded Indian chants add to the atmosphere.

The trail invites hikers to stroll at a leisurely pace, taking time to enjoy the scenery by sitting on benches along the way. One seating area is covered, providing a shady respite on a hot summer afternoon to study the well-written trail guide. This is an impressively large area. The mounds that now cover the rooms seem like ancient castle walls. Indeed, this place thrived in the 1200s. The high walls were used as protection against Comanche raids and probably were originally utilized as protection against other Pueblo people and Plains tribes.

The ruins of the old Catholic mission are the tallest structures remaining. Visitors can walk from the Native American pueblo to the remains of the mission. The walls of the two are similar. Another kiva—which contrasts the native religion with the creed brought from Europe—is located near the old Catholic mission. New research indicates that this kiva may have been constructed by a priest as a transitional room for instruction in Catholicism.

Albuquerque

A colorful old town nestled in the midst of malls, glass skyscrapers, and a bustling city, New Mexico's largest city contains many contrasts. Ancient cultures and history next to a burgeoning computer industry. Dry deserts, cottonwood-covered river bottoms, alongside towering mountain peaks filled with aspen, pine, and alpine ski areas. The variety, including museums and lodging, makes it a good place for families looking to take a break from camping and outdoor experiences and spend a day or two exploring. Sites like the Albuquerque Children's Museum, the Explora Science Center, Rio Grande Zoo, the American International Rattlesnake Museum, National Atomic Museum, Cliffs Amusement Park, Indian Pueblo Cultural Center, and New Mexico Museum of Natural History promise to entertain and inform young visitors.

Children often enjoy sipping on a soda or tasting a taco in Albuquerque's Old Town section. The city traces its roots back to this square, where Francisco Cuervo y Valdes first established a villa in 1706. A number of family-oriented outdoor and cultural opportunities are located within a 2-hour radius of Albuquerque. Some, like the Rio Grande Nature Center and Petroglyph National Monument, are located on the outskirts of town.

Camping is not allowed on national forest lands in the Sandia Mountains, which dominate the city skyline. Those who do camp can stay in commercial campgrounds on the edge of the city. Motel rooms in all price ranges are plentiful.

Coronado State Park

Located outside of the town of Bernalillo north of Albuquerque and off Interstate 25, this small state park serves as a quick—but extremely interesting—stop. It features a campground and day use area with covered picnic tables located along the banks of the Rio Grande River. The campground also has a playground for young campers. The park is within sight of a golf course operated by the Santa Ana tribe. While the small ruins complex at the park is similar to many in the Southwest, the interest here is some of the best preserved murals from a kiva in North America. These murals, displayed in a room adjacent to the visitor center, were removed during a 1930 excavation. The visitor center itself, designed by famous architect John Gaw Meem, is on the National Register of Historic Places. The center houses hands-on exhibits for children. Kids especially like grinding corn on a mano and metate, playing with drums, and examining the armor of a Spanish conquistador.

Coronado Ruins Trail

0.25 mile, loop, year-round

While there is no trail brochure to accompany visitors who

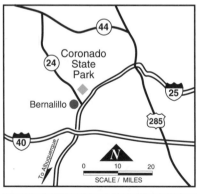

take the short walk through the ruins, signs along the way explain the significance of this area. Quotations from the journal of Spanish explorer Pedro de Castaneda, who came with Francisco Vasquez de Coronado in 1540, tell what the Spaniards discovered when they first arrived at this remote place on the banks of the Rio Grande River.

Coronado spent the winter of 1540 in the pueblo. He reached the spot with 300 soldiers, 1,000 Indian allies and slaves, 1,000 horses, and 500 mules. The area served as the conquistador's winter quarters before he set out in spring for the Great Plains in search of the fabled Seven Cities of Cibola. It was also a stopping point on his way back the next fall. Pedro de Castaneda describes scenes from the daily life of the native people who lived in the area. The women ground corn and played music on what he described as a fife. Another journalkeeper wrote that Pueblo women and men lived in complete equality with no sign of male authority.

The reconstructed walls of the pueblo outline the place where the rooms were located. Much of the original pueblo was made of an adobe brick that decomposed. Of special note is a rare reconstructed square kiva. This is where the murals in the visitor center were found and removed. The kiva has been reconstructed and duplications of the murals have been painted around its interior. The smooth stone floor and painted walls give it a more realistic look than found in similar Southwestern sites.

A child preparing to explore a kiva at Coronado State Park

The park also sheds light on what happened to other ancient cultures. It was occupied between 1300 and 1600 but abandoned at the beginning of the 1600s at the end of a twenty-year drought. There are records of periods of conflict with other tribes and with the Spaniards. The people of the modern Sandia and Santa Ana pueblos claim ancestral links to this Kuana Pueblo.

After completing the stroll around the ruins, hikers can take a short nature walk on a graveled trail along the Rio Grande River. The trail leads to three covered picnic tables.

Rio Grande Nature Center

When visiting the Southwest, many visitors hear about the legendary Rio Grande River. This noteworthy 270-acre nature center—operated by the New Mexico State Parks and Recreation Division—gives families a chance to experience the river and its natural systems. To reach the center, located in Albuquerque, drive west on Candelaria Boulevard off Interstate 25 or take Rio Grande Boulevard north of Interstate 40 until it intersects with Candelaria. The visitor center, a cement structure built into a berm, involves children in all sorts of natural experiences. A hands-on museum imparts chances to touch and feel the feathers and skins of many of the creatures that live in the Rio Grande Bosque. Built next to a 3-acre pond inhabited by waterfowl and turtles, the visitor center provides "portholes" of various shapes and sizes that allow children to "spy" on the wild creatures that use the pond. Park interpreters lead a children's hike Sundays at 11:00 A.M. A number of other family and educational activities are available throughout the year. A small bookstore with child-oriented materials as well as good guidebooks to the Southwest is also part of the visitor center.

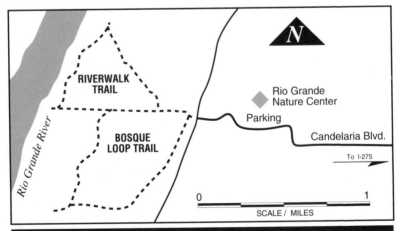

Riverwalk–Bosque Loop Trail

2 miles, loop, year-round

Starting from the visitor center, these two loop trails explore the river-bottom ecology of the Rio Grande, offering glimpses of the river as well as chances to see over 260 species of birds, an occasional mammal, and wildflowers. Both utilize trail guides obtained at the visitor center. Since the two trails join at one point, the numbered trail markers are color coded, depending on which route is chosen. Because both hikes are short, flat, easy, and focus on different ecology lessons, families may want to take both. Benches, which provide opportunities to watch quietly for birds or sketch in a journal, are plentiful on both trails. For children—as well as adults who grew up watching Wile E. Coyote and Roadrunner cartoons—the chance to actually see a roadrunner scurrying through the thicket makes these walks enticing. In fact, it is also possible to see a coyote.

Along the river at Rio Grande Nature Center

The Riverwalk Trail is a 1-mile loop that takes approximately 35 minutes to complete. As its name implies, the trail imparts information on the river system, introducing hikers to the natural systems that shaped the Albuquerque area. Some of the trail's best educational lessons center around showing how humans and their construction projects have shaped the ecology of the once natural riverbed. For those who want to walk along the Rio Grande and stick their feet in the river, the halfway point of this trail offers such an opportunity.

Every good hike should include a new word. The word on the Bosque Loop Trail is "bosque." According to park literature, a bosque is a riverside forest area consisting of native cottonwood trees and willows as well as non-native imports such as Russian olive and tamarisk. This loop trail covers 0.8 mile and takes about 20 minutes to complete. The tour guide encourages hikers to think, often not giving readily apparent answers. Look for human influences. Learn what non-native plants have done to this river environment. Search for evidence of animals and listen and watch for birds. Take time to discuss environmental ethics as a family. If not in the mood for learning, many children will simply enjoy looking for wildlife along the walk through the often shaded woods.

Sandia Mountain

To reach the National Scenic Byway leading up the back of Sandia Mountain, which guards the eastern side of Albuquerque, drive east on Interstate 40. Take the Tijeras exit, driving through the hamlet of Cedar Crest on New Mexico Highway 14. Drive on Highway 14 north past Cedar Crest to New Mexico 536, the Sandia Crest National Scenic Byway. There are a number of pleasant U.S. Forest Service picnic areas on the east side of the Sandias, but no overnight camping is permitted. At the top of the scenic highway at an elevation of 10,678 feet, visitors can enjoy a 360-degree view, which includes most of Albuquerque. The road dead ends at a small gift shop and restaurant at the top. Another way to view the area is to take a ride on the 2.7-mile Sandia Peak Tram—the longest in the U.S.—which can be reached by driving along Tramway Boulevard on the eastern edge of Albuquerque on the west side of the mountain.

Tree Springs Trail

2 miles, one-way, spring–fall

A trail marker and large parking lot mark the Tree Springs trailhead. There is also a pit toilet near the start of the trail. This slightly over 2-mile trail leads up a series of switchbacks in a steady uphill climb into the Sandia Mountain Wilderness and to a glorious view of Albuquerque. Because of some local vandalism problems at parking areas near U.S. Forest Service trailheads, it is a good idea to take your valuables with you.

Because the trek involves a bit of a climb, focus young hikers' attention on what will be happening around the next turn. This trail works its way up through different plant communities with wildflowers blooming nearly everywhere. At the start, this heavily traveled trail winds up through tall conifers and oak. At one point, it comes out into the open with more scrub oak and a view of the valley. But it soon returns to the conifer (spruce fir) forest for a short distance until it comes around to the sunny side of the mountain. Aspen mark the trail's entry into that plant zone.

Climbing farther through conifers again, hikers reach a sign pointing 1.5 miles one

A child getting a lift on the Tree Springs Trail

way to the tram house. There is another slightly confusing trail marker to the Crest Trail that shows two directions. Go straight ahead to the designated wilderness sign and then fork past that point to the left. The crest—with its rewarding view of Albuquerque and a few steep cliffs—is only a few hundred feet away.

Petroglyph National Monument

While petroglyphs can be found in almost every cliff dwelling site in the Four Corners region, nowhere can they be seen in such numbers as at Petroglyph National Monument. In fact, this small monument on Albuquerque's West Mesa holds one of the largest concentrations of rock art in North America. What makes it more interesting is that it does not seem to accompany a large habitation. Instead, the petroglyphs are chipped into large dark lava boulders in what seems to be an outdoor art gallery or church. Ask children to take pads of paper with them to sketch some of the designs they see. Avoid letting them trace or touch the actual rock art since that can damage these ancient writings. Ask children what they think the ancient people were trying to say. Perhaps young explorers can create their own symbols. These petroglyphs date from 1000 B.C. to recent times. In fact, travelers can view a pueblo of Kuana at nearby Coronado State Park that was inhabited by the same Pueblo Indians who produced much of the art at Petroglyph National Monument. The monument itself contains only 4 percent of the 15,000 or more petroglyphs along the volcanic escarpment. Management of the monument is shared by the Open Space Division of the city of Albuquerque and the National Park Service. The National Park Service's Las Imagines Visitor Center is located at 4735 Unser Boulevard NW.

Petroglyph Hiking Trails

Mesa Point Trail / 0.25 mile, Macaw Trail / 200 yards,
Cliff Base Trail / 600 yards, all one-way, year-round

There are three main trails—all short and easy for children—inside the monument. The entrance station to the main trail system at Boca Negra Canyon is open from 9:00 A.M. to 6:00 P.M. in the summer and from 8:00 A.M. to 5:00 P.M. in the winter. Visitors can obtain a trail brochure, enjoy a picnic, and ask questions. Use a loop road to access the trails.

The Mesa Point Trail, the longest in the canyon, takes about 30 minutes. This paved and well-marked trail winds up and around dark-colored volcanic boulders on a rather steep hill. While the brochure and trail markers point out obvious petroglyphs, many more can be found by careful observation. The mesa top itself is flat except for a low wall archaeologists suggest may have been part of an ancient ceremonial area. Views of Sandia Mountain to the east and the cinder cones of Albuquerque—where the lava flows originated—to the west reward hikers who make it to the top.

Follow the loop road to the next parking area, which serves as the trailhead for the two other trails.

The Macaw Trail is a short loop. It gets its name from unusual macaw petroglyphs. Ask children why ancient people drew pictures of macaws. Can these colorful birds be seen flying around the monument? No, but these birds were traded by prehistoric traders from the jungles of Mexico!

The short Cliff Base Trail covers easier-to-hike terrain than the Mesa Top Trail. Follow the markers to view more petroglyphs. Of interest are masks with elaborate headdresses. Have children study the forms of lava as well. Near the end of the trail are smooth spots worn into the lava by continued grinding of wild grass seed, pigments for coloring, and perhaps medicines with manos or grinding stones.

Longer hikes can be taken in outlying sections of the park. Rinconada Canyon 3 miles south on Unser Boulevard, Piedras Marcadas 4.5 miles north on Golf Course Road, or the West Side Volcanoes accessible via westbound I-40 and Paseo del Volcan are all good places to view more rock art. Hiking and road maps to these areas are available from rangers at either the visitor center or entrance station.

Acoma Pueblo

What happened to the Anasazi who lived in the Four Corners region? After children tour many of the ruin sites, that question is certain to surface. While archaeologists are not certain, some native people living in the region today claim to be the descendants. Visiting the Acoma Sky City, believed to be the oldest continuously inhabited city in the United States, certainly gives some validity to that theory. This ancient city, now inhabited by anywhere from two to thirteen families, depending on the season, sits on seventy acres at the top of a 370-foot-high mesa overlooking the desert. To reach the city, drive 55 miles west of Albuquerque on Interstate 40 to Exit 108 and then drive south on Highway 23. If driving east from Grants on Interstate 40, take Exit 96 and drive southeast on Highway 33 to Highway 38. Drivers will hit a junction with Highway 32 that leads directly to the visitor center. The Acoma operate a small gift shop, restaurant, and museum at the base of the Sky City. Since Acoma pottery is among the finest of its kind in the world, families may want to take along extra cash to either buy from vendors outside the visitor center or at the Sky City itself. The public is not allowed into Sky City without a tour guide. Tickets for tours are purchased at the visitor center. The pueblo's annual feast day is September 2, celebrating the Feast of San Esteban at Old Acoma with the Harvest Dance. Families in the area at that time should brave the crowds and enjoy a unique experience.

Sky City Tour

0.75 mile, round-trip,
year-round (0.75 mile one-way back from
Sky City to Visitor Center)

After purchasing tickets at the visitor center, families wait to take a bus up a paved road to the Sky City. Hikers must stay with a tour guide during the duration of the hour-long visit to the city. Those who want to buy pottery or other souvenirs from vendors in the old city must make their decisions quickly. The tour passes through the old streets only once.

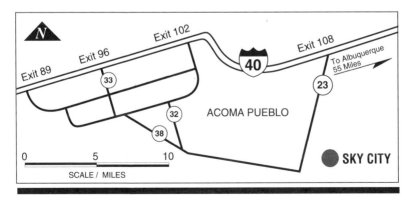

Stepping into this ancient city, which is believed to date back to 1150, is like walking from modern America into an ancient pueblo. Only a smattering of cars and trucks and an occasional television antenna break the feeling that this city belongs to another era. With square kivas, dusty streets, and pueblo-like architecture, walking through Sky City feels similar to spending time near a Mesa Verde cliff dwelling or a Chaco Canyon ruin. But there is a big difference. People live here.

A tour guide tells the story of Sky City, offering personal insights. Questions will certainly arise, and the native guides are more than willing to offer answers.

After walking the streets of the pueblo, the tour ends at the San Esteban del Rey Mission, an old adobe church. Construction of the church started in 1629 and was completed in 1640. The graveyard just outside the orange-walled mission allows fascinating glimpses at the combination of Christianity and native religions.

When the tour ends, visitors are invited to take the bus back to the visitor center or to walk the original route. If at all possible, take the walk. It leads through narrow sandstone passageways. Children will feel a sense of adventure as they climb down steep steps cut in stone, occasionally stopping to talk to native children along the way. Toward the end of the walk, hikers can stop in at some of the pottery shops along the road.

El Malpais National Monument

This national monument combines the interpretive efforts of the National Park Service and Bureau of Land Management and is an interesting mix of black lava flows and the tan, red, and buff-colored desert sandstone typical of the Southwest. Located off Interstate 40 and south of the town of Grants, the area includes mostly backcountry experiences with few facilities. Those who want to spend the night can find good lodging in Grants. Private campgrounds, national forest camping facilities, and camping at nearby El Morro National Monument are available. There is an information center in Grants, and for those who take Exit 89 off Interstate 40 and drive south 11 miles, there is a modern ranger station and a small but interesting museum with good interpretive exhibits. Hikers with good boots and a sense of adventure can explore lava tubes, ice caves, and largely untouched wilderness. Many of the hikes, however, are longer than families with young children enjoy. The charm of this monument is its sense of remoteness and wildness.

La Ventana Natural Arch Hike

0.5 mile, round-trip, year-round, snow is possible

This might be the easiest wilderness area a family will ever visit. Located about 12 miles south of the El Malpais Ranger Station on the east side of the road, the trailhead to New Mexico's largest natural arch is situated at the edge of the Cebolla Wilderness Area. Within a few feet of the parking areas, hikers encounter a sign telling them they are entering a wilderness.

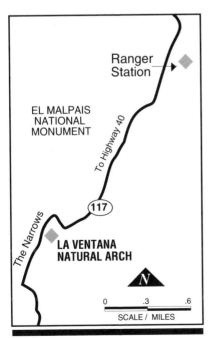

At first, the short trail that leads through pinyon/juniper forest is flat and dusty. As it begins to ascend to the base of towering La Ventana Arch, it starts to offer some easy challenges. As it climbs up sandstone steps, the trail leads to a little alcove directly under the arch.

There are places to sit in natural sandstone chairs while enjoying views of the alcove, arch, and valley below. It is possible to see the lava tube and nearby Mount Taylor. There is a natural grotto here where small pools allow lush green plants to grow in the largely desert environment. Notice the difference a bit of water makes in the types of plant communities that can survive in the desert. The area around the water is considerably cooler, allowing families in the middle of a long day's drive to sit for a while and enjoy a respite from the hot desert below.

A large natural amphitheater is located behind the arch. Canyon wrens dive from the top of the cliffs, breaking the silence of the desert.

El Morro National Monument

This national monument, located 125 miles west of Albuquerque, can be reached by driving southwest on New Mexico Highway 53 from Grants. A beautiful and remote nine-unit campground and two private recreational-vehicle parks near the entrance offer overnight accommodations. Lodging is available in Grants or Gallup. This is a place to contemplate the need of humans to leave their marks, both physical and historical. At El Morro, inscriptions on the prominent sandstone chronicle the history of the Southwest. The formation on the bluff, which is the dominant feature of this remote monument, led to a large collection of water, sometimes as much as 200,000 gallons, in a pond that served ancient people well. Here, Anasazi obtained water for their pueblos on top of the bluff. Spaniards on their way to colonize or convert natives to Christianity stopped here as well. So did railroad crews, California emigrants, and an experimental United States Army outfit called the Camel Corps. Many took time not only to refresh themselves, but to carve their names—and sometimes bits of poetry—on the soft sandstone walls next to ancient rock writing. The visitor center is home to a Junior Ranger program, a computer, and a touch table for children. A guidebook interprets the trail as do signs along the trail. A large rock is conveniently placed at the entrance to the visitor center so those who wish to sign their name in rock can do so without being tempted to deface the historical signatures on the trail.

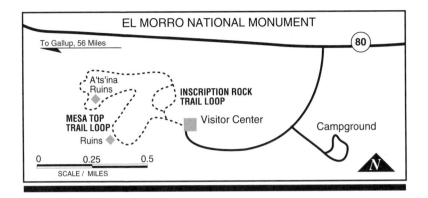

El Morro Hikes

0.5 mile or 2 miles, round-trip, year-round

Families who do not want to hike to the top of the bluff can take a short guided 0.5-mile trail that leads from the back of the visitor center to the ponds and rock inscriptions. A longer 2-mile trail—which most children will enjoy—leads to the mesa top with its small ruin and great views of the valley below. Another short option is to take the A'ts'ina Ruins Trail by hiking left where the trail splits and heading directly to the mesa top.

Parents of children who have visited other Anasazi sites can invite their kids to search for familiar petroglyph figures. Also, compare the "handwriting" styles of each of the people who signed the rock. The ancients, the Spanish, and the American visitors each had a particular style.

In many ways, the inscriptions on the sandstone wall represent the many battles over ownership of this barren land. Reminders of the Anasazi, Spaniards, and U.S. Army can be seen in close proximity, offering a glimpse and a timeframe of the area's history. Use these inscriptions—and information inside the visitor center—to talk about the settlement and history of New Mexico.

While viewing the inscriptions—some of which are amazingly intricate and poetic—hikers also pass the famous waterhole. There are no springs feeding this important oasis. Instead, rainwater from winter storms and summer thundershowers falls off the mesa and into this natural pool. With its deep green water and wetlands-type plant life contrasting with the sandstone cliffs, this is an enjoyable spot. Children and adults should resist the temptation to throw rocks in the pool.

After the last of the inscriptions, hikers can choose a trail back to the visitor center to complete the Inscription Rock Trail or can continue on to the mesa top. The trail to the top starts out fairly level and shaded by a pinyon/juniper forest. It includes a place against a sheer wall where children can hear a fine echo. The trail then rises, using eight short but steep switchbacks to the mesa top. From here, the trail is either carved out of the sandstone or marked by grooves on either side of the trail. In fact, the trail from this point seems to have been constructed by an inspired engineer who used stone steps, bridges, and railings to guide travelers over every rough spot. This makes the trail easy to follow and gives the kids an incentive to stay on the trail away from the steeper edges. There are views of the valley and mesa on one side and a sandstone box canyon on the other.

Looking at the A'ts'ina Ruins at the top of the mesa, hikers will likely be impressed with the great sense of aesthetics of the ancient people who inhabited this spot. Or, was this place perhaps built so the ancients could spot enemies coming from miles away in the distance? Only a corner of the ruins has been excavated, but the outline of the remaining pueblo—about the size of two city blocks—can be determined by looking for the raised mounds all around the mesa top. Of special interest are the two kivas. One is square, the other round. The question is why?

From A'ts'ina, the trail, carved into the sandstone, leads down the south side of the mesa and through a pinyon/juniper forest to the visitor center, on a loop trail.

Aztec Ruins National Monument

Located on the outskirts of the interesting little town of Aztec, Aztec Ruins National Monument provides the kind of short stop during a long desert drive that many families need. Unless a family stops for a picnic in the shaded picnic grounds at the monument or takes time to watch the movie presentation on the Anasazi in the visitor center and museum, the stop and short walk through the ruins will consume less than an hour of time, but it is time well spent. Also, children will be invited to pick up litter and make observations along the way in order to earn a Junior Ranger badge. Check at the visitor center for details on this program designed to encourage children to take a closer look at the ruins complex.

Aztec Ruins Hike

400 yards, round-trip, year-round

Though only about 400 yards long, the self-guided walk through the West Ruin—which archaeologists believe was constructed in the 1100s—provides one experience that cannot be duplicated anywhere in the Southwest. At first, the trail wanders along the outside of the ruins. Hikers can then walk inside one of the ruins, getting glimpses of roof construction. At the visitor center pick up a well-done trail guide that will enhance your visit greatly.

The trail ends at a reconstructed "Great Kiva," the only fully reconstructed great kiva in the Southwest. Since the circular room is believed to have served as a ceremonial place for the ancient people who once resided here, the feeling of walking through the entrance is not unlike visiting a European cathedral. There is a tendency to want to talk in whispers and show reverence. Lit by an opening in the ceiling, the dark, dusty space enchants and sparks new interest among children, leading to many questions. Those queries can often be answered by reading the trail brochure. The soft sounds of a Zuni sunrise chant fill the large, impressive-looking room. As in church, older hikers may want to simply pick a quiet spot to sit and contemplate the past. How was the structure built? What was it used for? Why was it abandoned? The atmosphere of this place invites those questions, allowing hikers to enjoy a colorful part of Southwest history and to come away inspired.

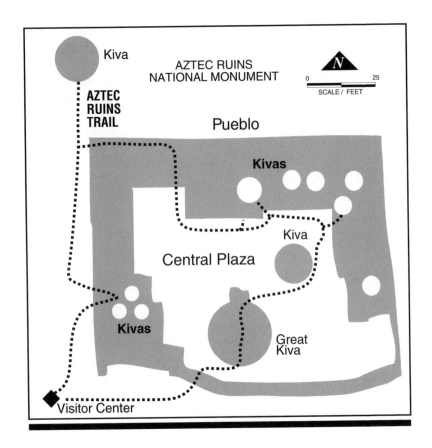

Chaco Canyon
National Historical Park

The road leading to Chaco Canyon National Historical Park is dirt and can make for difficult travel. However, crossing the dusty, bumpy road is well worth it. Chaco is considered one of the premier archaeological sites in the Southwest. Visitors can drive south on Highway 44, then turn off 44 at Nageezi and follow San Juan County Road for 11 miles to New Mexico 57. Another route travels north onto New Mexico 57 from I-40 at Thoreau and goes 44 miles on paved road. North of Crownpoint 2 miles, New Mexico 57 turns to the right (east) to a marked turnoff. From there a 20-mile stretch of unpaved road heads north to the visitor center. Call 505-786-7014 or 505-786-7060 (emergency number) to inquire about road conditions. Either way, travelers will face a long and bumpy 20- to 26-mile drive over a dusty dirt road. Since there are no food, gas, lodgings, or auto repair services available at the park, travelers must come prepared to camp at the 64-unit Gallo Campground 1 mile east of the park visitor center. Camping is allowed on a first-come, first-served basis, so arrive as early in the day as possible during the busy spring and summer seasons. The best lodgings are found at Aztec to the north or Grants to the south, but they are a good distance away.

A visitor pauses near an interpretive sign at Chaco Canyon.

Since Chaco is located in a desert environment at 6,200 feet, expect to find extremes in temperatures. It is not unusual for the temperature to change 40 degrees on a single summer day, from a high close to 100 degrees Fahrenheit to nighttime lows around 60.

Families who brave the difficulties of the journey are rewarded with relatively easy hikes, a fascinating visitor center, and an unforgettable experience. There are five self-guided trails in Chaco, all with trail brochures. A few longer day hikes also offer impressive views from the tops of slickrock canyons down into what is believed to be a major center for the Anasazi culture from about A.D. 900 until A.D. 1180. Hiking trails are only open from sunrise to sunset. This regulation is strictly enforced, so plan hikes accordingly. Trailheads are located along a paved one-way loop road that begins and ends at the visitor center.

Archaeologists can only speculate on the number of people who lived in this place. Population estimates range from as high as 10,000, when Neill Judd identified the structures as apartment complexes, to as few as 2,000 residents. Over 4,000 archaeological sites have been identified in and around the impressive canyon, which seems to open up out of nowhere when driving across the flat desert. The park is so significant that it has been designated as a World Heritage Site. Because of the fragile nature of the ruins and the number of artifacts still scattered about the desert, before taking their first hike parents should carefully review the section on ethics at archaeological sites found in the introduction of this book.

Pueblo Bonito

0.6 mile, loop, year-round

The most famous site in Chaco Canyon is this 600-room, four-story-high structure, which shows the skill of the ancient people who inhabited this desolate area and the majesty of the architecture. Though the trail distance is short, much can be seen. An 18-stop self-guided trail brochure is helpful, but families who can sign up for a ranger-guided tour should take advantage of the opportunity.

There is a feeling of quiet in the canyon for Chaco is removed from the sounds of modern society. On a cool desert morning, just

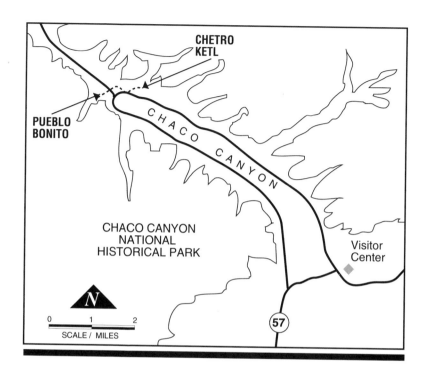

after the sun has risen, there is a tendency to whisper or to remain silent and contemplative. There is a feel of old spirits in the air, spirits of past inhabitants.

Walking along the back of this impressive structure, where walls as high as four stories remain, provides families with an idea as to the complexity of this massive structure. Take time to examine the intricate stonework used to construct the walls and note the changes in the masonry styles as the complex grew.

Though located next to a canyon cliff, Pueblo Bonito is not a cliff dwelling like families have seen at Mesa Verde National Park in Colorado. Instead, the pueblo is constructed at the base of an impressive-looking canyon wall.

There is an air of mystery about this place. Because the ancients left no written record, archaeologists can only speculate about many aspects of the lives of these people. Parents should use the trail brochure to ask their children to offer their own theories about this special place.

Chetro Ketl

0.6 mile, loop, year-round

This self-guided trail leads hikers through sections of excavated and unexcavated ruins as part of an ancient pueblo. It is estimated that Chetro Ketl contained 500 rooms and 16 kivas, including one of the largest great kivas in the Chaco complex. There is a slight elevation gain on the 0.6-mile gravel trail but, like most Chaco trails, families should have little trouble enjoying this walk.

On this hike, parents can talk to their children about the difficulty of building with wooden blocks and interlocking building blocks at home. A child who has struggled to construct a free-standing structure with a set of wooden blocks can then look at the rock and masonry construction so evident in Chetro Ketl. By relating the building of Chetro Ketl to something a child knows, an impression might be made as to the difficulty ancient people had in building their homes. Like a child building with wooden blocks, these people had few modern tools to work with. Instead, they relied on their building skills. The trail brochure for this hike emphasizes the types of building materials used and the method of construction.

Chaco Canyon ruins have impressive masonry walls.

Utah

Families visiting southern Utah for the first time have an unfortunate tendency to lump all the wide open spaces together. In this domain of incredible diversity, that inclination is a mistake. It is possible, in the course of a single day, without traveling great distances, to ski at Brian Head in the morning, golf at St. George in the afternoon, and take an evening hike to an arch or through a lava tube at Snow Canyon State Park.

This is a region of contrasts. Deserts sit a few miles from alpine meadows. Tiny rural hamlets can be found only a short distance from one of the fastest-growing urban areas in the United States. It is a place of deserts carved by mighty rivers, of improbable landscapes and inconceivable beauty.

Just because the area's five national parks—Capitol Reef, Zion, Arches, Bryce, and Canyonlands—are located in the Colorado Plateau, do not be fooled into thinking they are similar. They are not. Bryce and Zion, located only 86 miles apart, are as different as Yellowstone and the Grand Canyon.

Do not be afraid to explore the region's smaller national monuments, state parks, or vast Bureau of Land Management and U.S. Forest Service property. Some of these places offer unique experiences found nowhere else in the world, such as taking a commercial four-wheel-drive adventure, rafting down the Green or Colorado river, or riding a mountain bike across desert slickrock.

Some families make the mistake of trying to cover too much of southern Utah in too little time and end up spending their entire vacation driving. Use this guide to help break a Utah vacation into smaller regions. One time, for example, concentrate on a trip to the Bryce Canyon–Zion–Cedar Breaks area in southwestern Utah. On another trip, visit Capitol Reef National Park with stops at Lake Powell and Goblin Valley State Park. Base a trip in Moab, Green River, Blanding, or Monticello in the southeastern portion of the state, visiting Canyonlands and Arches national parks and Hovenweep and Natural Bridges national monuments.

Whatever your choice, touring southern Utah brings the promise of adventure, diversity, and world-class scenic beauty to family travelers.

St. George–Cedar City

Though located a mere 60 miles apart off Interstate 15, Cedar City and St. George offer visitors to southwestern Utah two distinctive urban areas and climates.

At an elevation of 5,800 feet and located in the midst of a pinyon/juniper forest, Cedar City's climate has four distinct seasons. This city of 13,500 is, in many ways, a college town shaped by the presence of Southern Utah University. The school is the cultural center of the area, offering a variety of concerts, plays, and athletic events. Of great interest to traveling families is the annual Utah Shakespearean Festival, which uses one outdoor and two indoor theaters—the former a replica of Shakespeare's Globe—to present six plays that run simultaneously from the first week of July through the first week of September. Though older children may enjoy the cultural experience of attending a play, especially in the outdoor theater, families with small children should stop by to enjoy the free Greenshow playing nightly except Sundays on the university grounds surrounding the outdoor theater. Puppeteers, falconers, dancers, and storytellers dressed in Victorian costumes use several small stages and the grassy areas to present skits, dances, music, and fables. In many cases, they also interact with the audience.

Iron Mission State Park, located on Main Street, is another enjoyable family destination in Cedar City. It contains a number of historical carriages and stagecoaches, including one reportedly shot by Butch Cassidy. Families will learn about the iron mines established by settlers to this area. Skiers can enjoy downhill runs at the Brian Head ski resort located up Cedar Canyon adjacent to Cedar Breaks National Monument.

Driving south on Interstate 15 to St. George, travelers will notice a distinct change in the climate and the scenery. At an elevation of 2,880 feet, this booming city of 30,000 residents is in one of the fastest-growing counties in the United States. Early settlers, who came here from Salt Lake City in an attempt to grow cotton in the warm climate, called the area Utah's "Dixie," a monicker that remains today. There are eight golf courses in the St. George area, making it a popular winter destination. Families also enjoy visiting sites like the Jacob Hamblin Home in nearby Santa Clara and Brigham Young's winter home in St. George.

Because of their size and close proximity to national parks like Zion, Bryce, and the Grand Canyon, Cedar City and St. George contain fine motels, restaurants, campgrounds, shopping opportunities, and recreational-vehicle parks.

Zion National Park

As the most popular of Utah's five national parks, Zion accords families many opportunities to enjoy its impressive canyons, checkerboard mesas, and outstanding backcountry. There are three entrances to the park. Most visitors use the south entrance, 60 miles south of Cedar City on Utah Highway 9 near Zion Canyon. That is where the large Watchman and South campgrounds, the main visitor center, and the Zion Nature Center can be found. At least a few loops of the Watchman Campground are open year-round. Both camping facilities open during the busy May through September season at Zion and often fill early. Because reservations are not accepted for camping, plan on arriving early. Though there are flush toilets and running water at these campgrounds, showers are only available at private campgrounds located outside the park's east and south entrances.

Throughout the year, park rangers conduct a variety of interpretive activities including evening programs at Zion Lodge and campground amphitheaters, guided hikes, and patio talks. Programs are offered on a limited basis in January and February. An

Hikers in Zion Canyon

impressive multimedia slide show at the visitor center serves as a good introduction to the park. The visitor center also features a small museum and bookstore with materials on the natural and human history of the area. Rangers are on hand to answer questions. A 2.5-mile bicycle trail leads from Watchman Campground into Zion Canyon. The Junior Ranger program at Zion is one of the best in the country. The program operates from Memorial Day through Labor Day at the Zion Nature Center north of the South Campground and is for children six to twelve years of age. Daily sessions run from 9:00 to 11:30 A.M. and 1:30 to 4:00 P.M., with registration prior to each session. It is worth checking out, especially if mom and dad need a short break from the kids. Zion Lodge, located in Zion Canyon, is open year-round, providing visitors with motel units, cabins with fireplaces, a restaurant, snack bar, and gift shop. Families also enjoy taking a guided horseback ride, available from late March through early November each year. The corral is located near Zion Lodge.

Visitors can drive up increasingly crowded Zion Canyon for views of the park. The road dead ends at the mouth of the Zion Narrows near the trailhead for the Riverside Walk. Parking lots sometimes fill, so consider taking a ride aboard an open air tram operated out of Zion Lodge.

Kids will especially enjoy taking the Zion–Mt. Carmel Highway. The road, completed in 1930, takes visitors from the canyon floor to the top through two narrow tunnels, including one that is 1.1 miles long. Expect some delays in the summer when traffic is occasionally stopped to allow motor homes to go through the tunnels. This road leads to the park's east entrance and US 89 and is a popular route for travelers heading to Bryce Canyon, the Grand Canyon, or the Glen Canyon National Recreation Area. The other park entrance is located in the Kolob Canyons area on the north end of the park right off Interstate 15. There is a small visitor center at this entrance. The road leads to a picnic area and overlooks the Kolob Canyons area of the park.

The Zion Canyon area features seven major day hikes and numerous backcountry routes. There are also two long day hikes starting at Kolob Canyons, including an 8-hour all-day adventure to Kolob Arch. The town of Springdale at the south entrance offers bed and breakfast accommodations, gift shops, lodging, restaurants, and an IMAX movie called "Treasure of the Gods," partially filmed in the park.

Zion National Park is Utah's most popular national park.

Riverside Walk

2 miles, round-trip, year-round, can get snow

The trailhead for this easy but spectacular walk along the Virgin River at the gateway to the Zion Narrows is located at the end of Zion Canyon Scenic Drive. Plan on at least 1.5 hours to enjoy this easy stroll. However, because of the beauty of the high red-walled canyons, moss ferns and flowers of the hanging gardens, and lure of riverside beaches, this is an easy place to spend more time.

This paved trail receives heavy year-round use. At its start, National Park Service workers constructed a split rail fence to control foot traffic and preserve streamside vegetation. Turnouts along the way periodically allow access to the Virgin River and its cottonwood bottomlands. Small rock walls along portions of the trail protect young children at spots where the trail edges drop off. It is not unusual to see parents using strollers on this easy, fairly level trail (the elevation gain is only 57 feet).

Look up at the ribbon of blue sky that mirrors its twin, the river. Take time to listen to the sound of the river bouncing off the walls as the canyon begins to narrow. Watch for a rock room with a shallow pool to the right of the trail. From this point, the

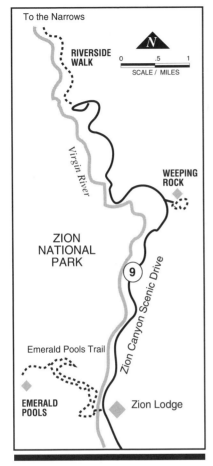

end of the trail and the entrance to the Zion Narrows is not far ahead.

When hikers reach the Narrows, the pavement ends. Hikers can wade into the river and peer up at the 20-foot-wide canyon cut straight through 1,000-foot-high walls. The 1- to 5-hour-long day hike up the Narrows should not be attempted by anyone under 4'8" because of deep pools and strong currents and the fact that throughout the Narrows there is no trail other than the riverbed. Since the depth of the water can change hourly, hikers should check with rangers before walking too far up the canyon. The longer all-day 16-mile hike from Chamberlain Ranch requires a permit that can be obtained at the visitor center starting at 5:00 P.M. the night before. Do not be surprised if cold water or the potential for flash flooding close the route. A few overnight backcountry permits are available for those wanting to make the trip in two days.

Emerald Pools Trail

1.2 miles to Lower Pool, 2 miles to Middle Pool, 3 miles to Upper Pool, all round-trip, year-round, can get snow

The hike to Lower, Middle, and Upper Emerald pools can begin either from Zion Lodge or from the Emerald Pools trailhead east of the lodge. The Sand Bench Trail, an easy flat walk on the east side of the Virgin River, also begins at this point.

Families with young children may want to attempt the easy 1.2-mile round-trip paved walk to Lower Pool. If energy remains, they can complete the 2-mile loop hike to Middle Pool. When Middle Pool is reached, older children or families with veteran hikers may want to walk another 0.33 mile up a rugged trail to the impressive Upper Pool located under massive vertical cliffs.

Begin the walk by using the sturdy steel and wood plank bridge to cross the Virgin River. Though it is a loop trail, signs at the beginning indicate that hikers heading for Upper and Middle pools head left and those interested in Lower Pool go right. For hikers planning to do the entire loop, the choice of directions does not matter.

The paved lower trail involves a gentle but steady uphill climb through a shady scrub oak forest. There are steep dropoffs on one side of the trail at times as it climbs to the pools. Hikers enjoy first-class views of Zion Canyon along the way. The paved trail ends at Lower Pool, which has been fenced to protect the streamside vegetation. In fact, to protect the aquatic wildlife and preserve the area, swimming, wading, and bathing are prohibited in all three pools.

At this point, those who want to continue to Middle Pool must hike under an overhanging alcove behind Lower Pool. Except in the most dry times of year, families will also thrill to walking under at least two—and sometimes more after a recent storm—waterfalls. In the hot late spring and summer months, getting drenched can be a welcome experience. The trail then winds its way up through a narrow canyon. There are two points where hikers looking for a longer trip can head north toward the Grotto Picnic Area.

Upon reaching Middle Pool on a windy day, hikers marvel at the tricks the wind plays with the fine spray. This spot also gives hikers a chance to study the massive sandstone cliffs rising from the canyon floor and to trace the path water must take to make its way from top to bottom, sometimes spilling through large natural funnels gouged into the stone. The water sometimes seeps through cracks. At other times, it flows in sheets over the edge, leaving telltale streaks called desert varnish.

Once at Middle Pool, hikers can choose to take another 0.33-mile (one-way) trail spur to Upper Pool. The trail here is rocky and somewhat steep. It also branches off many times. The

Winter brings out children's creativity.

National Park Service has tried to discourage these mini-trails by putting logs or rocks across them. Hikers can protect the fragile desert environment by staying on the main trail. This spur should be fun for children over six years of age because it is short but challenging. Trees are close to the narrow trail, so children being carried on their parents' backs might not fare as well. Entering the Upper Pool area brings out the child in almost everyone. The tall sandstone cliffs that surround the large pool dwarf humans who can get cramped necks by bending back to see the top of the canyon. The sound of water, cultivating the hanging gardens on the surrounding walls, can be heard everywhere. Though the pools are tempting places to play or swim, ask children to resist the temptation in order to protect the fragile ecosystem. Hikers return to Middle Pool on the same narrow trail. At Middle Pool, hikers can either return to Lower Pool under the waterfalls or continue the loop, with different views of Zion Canyon, while ending at the same place.

Watchman Trail

2 miles, round-trip, year-round, can get snow

This short hike is a quick way to get an overview of Zion Canyon to the north or Springdale to the south. The trail can be hot during the summer. It is especially beautiful in early morning or late afternoon. Beware of rattlesnakes. Since the trailhead is located on the service road just east of the Watchman Campground, it is easily accessible by families camping at Zion. To reach the trailhead, drive across the bridge over the Virgin River and take the road to the left.

There is a box at the trailhead where hikers can pick up cards for natural history field observation. The Park Service uses these cards to encourage hikers to look for wildlife and to write detailed descriptions. The trail winds uphill all the way until near the top,

where a loop trail extends out around the top of a bench area. Take time to listen to the rustling of the cottonwood trees along the canyon bottom. Notice the many signs of abuse where hikers have ventured off the trail and rangers have tried to revegetate the area. Look for what such abuse can do. Erosion that washes away plants, exposes tree roots, and cuts deep scars hurts the land.

Search out signs of what a powerful force water can be. A small wash along the trail runs through dark red sand, and yet the sand at the bottom of the wash is almost white.

Look far ahead and up high to see the matching colors of rock layers that were the origin of this sand.

The trail proceeds up a side canyon. Look for signs of contrast. These include the large flat paddles of beavertail cactus that store water. A few yards away, cattails and other water-loving plants enjoy a trickle of water in the midst of this desert environment.

The trail works its way uphill to where hikers can see a series of switchbacks. Some young children may get bored at this point. Maintain their interest by pointing out the different layers of rock found along the trail. Discover petrified mud cracks, solid broad layers sitting on top of less resistant, rapidly eroding layers. Look for pack rat middens full of juniper leaves and berries left by these nocturnal creatures. Be careful not to touch these middens, however, because the rodents may carry diseases that are preserved in the debris piles.

The trail has rock walls built at points of sheer dropoffs. Youngsters who complete the hike will feel a sense of accomplishment as they look down at the tiny cars and people at the bottom of the trail.

Hikers then head west around smooth, eroded slopes to where the trail splits into a loop. To the right is the direct route to the Watchman lookout with views of Zion Canyon, the visitor center, and nearby Springdale. The loop trail branches out on a flat point where hikers can see the next canyon and returns to the trail's end.

Dixie Red Cliffs

There are three short hikes near the Bureau of Land Management's Dixie Red Cliffs campground. Located just west of the town of Leeds between Cedar City and St. George, this is a small scenic area that families easily miss on their way to Zion or the Grand Canyon. The Dixie Red Cliffs Campground is a loop consisting of eleven individual campsites with covered tables and a picnic area near Quail Creek. Quail Creek Reservoir—a Utah state park—is located downstream a few miles and features fine fishing, boating, and campgrounds. Three short hiking trails start at the Dixie Red Cliffs Campground.

Red Cliffs Nature Trail

0.5 mile, one-way, year-round

What was once a self-guiding nature trail has fallen into disrepair, largely due to vandalism. While the BLM has removed most of the signposts and no longer interprets the natural area, the easy and fairly well-marked trail is the kind of place where a family could spend the better part of a day. Huge cottonwoods offer shade. Cool water from Quail Creek and plenty of red sandstone beckon hikers.

The trailhead is found across from the picnic parking lot. It is the first trail those driving into the one-way loop road will see. A map outlining the trails is located at the campground entrance. There is a pack-it-in/pack-it-out policy on this trail. Hikers are encouraged to leave their refuse in campground dumpsters.

A slight incline starts the hike, but it soon levels out. Look for a huge, gnarled cottonwood to the right of the trail, behind a human-high boulder. Investigate the area behind the tree and discover it is hollow! It is a living cave. Kids enjoy hiding inside the giant trunk.

About 40 feet farther on the trail is a sandstone cave of relatively the same dimensions. Compare the sensations of both places. Look for cholla cactus, rare in Utah and more common in Arizona's deserts.

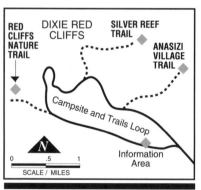

Benches are placed intermittently on this trail. The first bench is tucked back under an oak just before the trail descends into a small wash and goes up the other side. Several paths enter and exit here but reunite farther on. Metal posts mark the established trail.

As the trail reaches the creek once again, there are

wonderful places to stop, including a huge boulder on the left shaped like the bow of a ship. Search the creekbed for different kinds of sandstone. Some are pimply, some smooth, some red or yellow or buff.

At one point the trail splits into three forks. The right leads down to the creek. Here, a small waterfall tumbles over hard smooth rock to an inviting pool. The middle path is the most dangerous, as it traverses the rocks overlooking the falls area, and it has a hole by the trail that is child-size. The marked trail moves to the left, winding around the falls area and ending up at the creek again. This seems to be the end of the dry trail. Hikers may choose to turn back here or work their way up the canyon in the water or back and forth across the creek. Not a bad way to spend a hot summer day!

Dixie Red Cliffs is a fun place to hike.

Silver Reef Trail

0.12 mile, loop, year-round

The Silver Reef Trail, located on the northern end of the campground, is an adventure. A marker at its start warns that it is dangerous, and it could be, especially to those not used to hiking in sandstone and to children younger than eight. At one point, a cable railing marks the trail and lends support to those crossing the sandstone slanted at a 30-degree angle. Right at the end of the cable, look for dull red paint on the rock, marking the trail that bears to the right around a wall. The end of the trail is marked by more cable railing, protecting visitors from approximately a 15-foot dropoff. The viewpoint looks out over the Silver Reef ghost town, Quail Creek Reservoir, and the distant mesas.

Do not be afraid to drive over to the ghost town after your hike. Kids enjoy walking through a restored building housing an interesting little museum that explains the area's mining history.

Children looking at the Anasazi village at Dixie Red Cliffs

Anasazi Village Trail

0.2 mile, loop, year-round

Within sight of the trail back from Silver Reef Trail is the Anasazi Village Trail. This walk leads to a partially excavated Anasazi ruin. The smaller storage rooms are protected by a cover. This archaeological site is the northernmost extension of the Anasazi culture of the Four Corners region. Where once there were several hundred Virgin River Anasazi sites, only a dozen remain. Interpretive signs help families understand the historical significance of this ruin and others in the area.

Snow Canyon State Park

Located 13 miles north of St. George off Utah Highway 18, Snow Canyon State Park is one of the rare Colorado Plateau attractions that is more popular in winter than summer. Its mild winter climate makes it an ideal place to enjoy a February or March camping vacation. Summer temperatures, however, often reach into the 100s. A campground with showers, hook-ups, and covered patio for group use makes Snow Canyon a sought-after camping destination. The red sandstone scenery contrasts with black volcanic rock for a dramatic effect. Children enjoy playing in a fine pink sand dune found inside the park as well as rock scrambling near the campground. A horseback-riding concessionaire gives family travelers another way to enjoy the park. There are a number of easy hikes inside Snow Canyon. In the middle of the day, families can consider taking the short drive to the town of Veyo to enjoy a dip in Veyo Hot Springs, a 1930s vintage resort. Children tired of hiking also use a grassy area, basketball standards, volleyball facilities, and horseshoe pits near the campground.

A child examining a pothole at Snow Canyon State Park

Lava Caves

3,820 feet, one-way, mid-May through September

One of the most interesting aspects of Snow Canyon State Park is its close proximity to volcanoes. The combination of red and tan sandstones with dark basalt formations can be a photographer's dream. Hikers with a sense of adventure can explore a small lava cave—a tube formed by flowing volcanic lava.

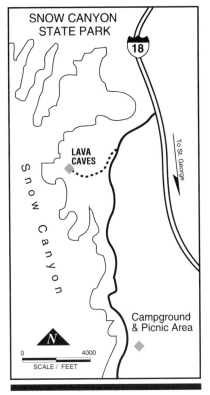

The hike begins on the Snow Canyon road just after it winds its way into the canyon from Utah 18. Driving south from that point, look for the trailhead sign on the right (west).

After a 0.75-mile hike, the entrances to three lava caves will be somewhat obvious. Families planning to explore the caves will need a good source of light (a gas lantern or two or three reliable flashlights are recommended) and a good pair of boots. The first cave entrance hikers will notice offers the best chance for exploration. Younger children will need help negotiating the jagged rocks and somewhat steep entrance.

There, hikers can determine how far back they can hike in the darkness. These are small lava caves compared to others, but the chance to explore a dark unknown more than makes up for the shortness of the tube.

Continue hiking another 0.25 mile past the lava tube entrances to enjoy a splendid view of West Canyon below.

Coral Pink Sand Dunes State Park

Located 27 miles northwest of Kanab on the Utah-Arizona border, scenic Coral Pink Sand Dunes State Park is a less crowded and more enjoyable camping alternative for travelers driving

Footprints in the sand at Coral Pink Sand Dunes State Park

between Zion, Bryce, and Grand Canyon national parks. Its small campground contains hot-water restrooms with showers. There is a boardwalk overlook trail and a 0.5-mile nature trail starting at the picnic area that helps interpret the area. The huge sand dunes made of fine pink sand offer acres of fun. Children love playing in the sand, climbing up and rolling down the dunes, or burying themselves in the fine, powdery sand. Though some areas are blocked off, the dunes are popular with off-highway-vehicle users, so families should be careful when playing in dunes.

Cedar Breaks National Monument

Located 23 miles east of Cedar City at an elevation of 10,000 feet, Cedar Breaks National Monument is primarily a summer destination. With wildflowers blooming in high alpine meadows from late June until August, that is a glorious time to visit. Visitor services are only available in the park from late May through mid-October when snow closes the park road. The visitor center opens on Memorial Day weekend, with ranger services available through Columbus Day in October.

However, do not let the heavy winter snows discourage a visit. The nearby Brian Head downhill ski resort offers year-round accommodations. A cross-country ski center at the resort helps to groom and mark trails on national forest lands between Brian Head and the monument. In addition, the National Park Service marks two cross-country ski trails inside the park. These include the North Rim Trail, a 1-mile loop that begins where Highway 143 crosses the park's north boundary at the Rattlesnake Creek trailhead, about 2 miles south of the Brian Head city limits. Interpreters recommend the trail for novice skiers. It leads to two overlooks and a small stand of bristlecone pines and through forests of spruce and fir along the north rim of the Cedar Breaks amphitheater. The other marked ski trail follows the route of the Alpine Pond Trail loop (see hike below). Park rangers say the upper portion of this trail is suitable for beginners. Relatively flat, it allows some views of the Breaks. Only expert skiers should try the Lower Alpine Pond Trail.

A groomed snowmobile trail, which can be skied, is maintained along the unplowed portion of Highway 148 along the canyon rim. Snowmobile rentals are available in the town of Brian Head.

Though the rock formations at Cedar Breaks may not be as intricate as nearby Bryce Canyon, the amphitheater—which is 2,000 feet deep and more than 3 miles in diameter—is slightly larger. The monument's small campground often fills in the summer, but there are U.S. Forest Service-managed facilities nearby at Panguitch and Navajo lakes and Cedar Canyon. A 5-mile road leads to four overlooks. The small visitor center is located near Point Supreme.

Alpine Pond Trail

2 miles, round-trip, spring–fall

Start this easy loop trail at either the Chessmen parking area

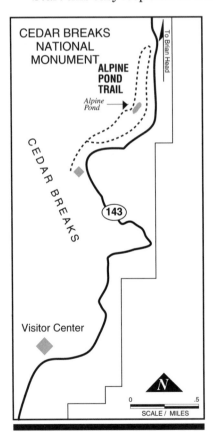

or the Alpine Pond parking area. Families not in the mood for such a long hike can have one adult shuttle the car between the two lots or trade keys along the way. This is an excellent hike on which to introduce children to alpine trees and flowers such as bristlecone and limber pines, Englemann spruce, aspens, lupine, dwarf mistletoe, and mountain bluebells. A trail guide is available to help in this regard. The hike is especially enjoyable from late June until August when wildflower displays hit their peaks.

Down the trail 0.5 mile, hikers get a chance to ponder the beauty of Cedar Breaks as they walk along the rim. Children may wonder why there are different colored rocks in the coliseum-like chasm below them. National Park

Service geologists say the rocks are layered because they were formed from sediments that collected at the bottom of a lake 65 million years ago. At times, snow banks may linger until August near the shady portion of the trail.

Faulting in the limestone subsurface created the Alpine Pond. While the pond serves as a collecting basin for rain, it is fed by a spring that runs year-round, eventually draining into Rattle Creek, one of the main water courses that help to sculpt the amphitheater through erosion of the sediments. In the early morning or late evening hours, hikers sometimes see such wildlife as mule deer.

Fremont Indian State Park

Located just off Interstate 70, 24 miles southwest of Richfield in Clear Creek Canyon, Fremont Indian State Park celebrates the culture of the Fremont Indians, who are believed to have disappeared about 800 years ago. According to park rangers, some archaeologists believe they are related to desert tribes that lived in the Mesa Verde–Chaco Canyon area. Others believe they were a branch of pueblo-dwelling people who migrated into the area. The state park consists of a campground, a museum, a reconstructed Fremont pit house, and twelve relatively short and easy hikes, some leading to rock art panels. Children may especially enjoy a museum exhibit that asks them to be archaeologists who study the past and the future. After being asked for theories on what different tools and rock writings collected from ancient peoples meant, visitors examine a modern child's bedroom, complete with toys and conveniences. What will scientists studying twentieth-century culture hundreds of years from now theorize about the uses of these toys? The hands-on museum is designed to produce some thought-provoking discussions.

A reconstructed pit house at Fremont Indian State Park

Parade of Rock Art—Court of Ceremonies—Canyon Overlook Trail

1.8 miles, round-trip, year-round

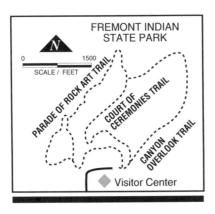

Though these are listed in park guidebooks as three separate trails, they are linked together to form a loop trail that begins and ends at the visitor center. The Parade of Rock Art Trail is 0.3 mile long and accessible by wheelchairs. It leads to some impressive rock art panels. Court of Ceremonies is 0.5 mile and leads to walls lined with human figures. Finishing the trail from that point is the 1-mile Canyon Overlook Trail with views of the canyon below. A side trip to the reconstructed pithouse leads back to the visitor center.

The trails wind through a small red rock canyon. The rock art should be obvious, but have children study the sandstone walls carefully to find the less conspicuous ancient writing. Since no one is quite certain what the meaning of the rock art is, families can discuss their own personal feelings about what the "authors" and "artists" who created the art were trying to say. Is this artwork, a map, or a written record? Because human contact can erase, mar, and destroy these ancient etchings, look but do not touch. Some children like to take a nature journal and to copy the rock art with their own interpretations.

Capitol Reef National Park

Located on Utah Highway 24 between the towns of Torrey and Hanksville, this increasingly popular national park is about a 4-hour drive south of Salt Lake City. There is no lodging inside the park, but accommodations are available in nearby towns. Fruita Campground, with 70 sites, is located in an historic orchard. Expect to see mule deer, chukars, and skunks in and around the camping area. A group site can also be reserved. The campground fills almost every day from April through mid-October. Loop A has a heated restroom that is winterized, making the campground ideal for a winter trip. U.S. Forest Service campgrounds on nearby Boulder Mountain off Highway 12 offer a fine alternative, especially during the hot summer months. The more remote Cathedral Valley and Cedar Mesa campgrounds are free primitive facilities with pit toilets and no water. Both are approximately 30 miles from the visitor center on a dirt road.

An historic blacksmith shop and one-room schoolhouse add to the charm of this park. The visitor center, which is open year-round, features a small museum, slide show, and bookstore. From early July into October, visitors may pick fruit in the historic orchards. While small amounts of fruit can be enjoyed for free, some fees are set for visitors wanting to pick larger amounts or to take fruit with them. This is an excellent place to introduce children to hiking with most of the 15 major short trails under 4 miles (round-trip). Some of the most popular hikes for children include Grand Wash, Hickman Bridge, and Capitol Gorge.

Fremont River Trail

1.25 miles, one-way, year-round

This short trail, which leads west from the Fruita Campground's amphitheater, delivers a great introduction to this land of red rock and spectacular scenery for late-arriving campers. Once it leaves the campground, the 1.25-mile hike winds along the Fremont River before becoming strenuous. The elevation gain of 730 feet could be tiring to some younger family members. The climb passes steep dropoffs so parents need to watch children closely. Since there is no definite destination other than a pile of rocks and a sign at the end of the trail, families can feel free to turn back any time the kids get tired.

The hike begins near the amphitheater parking area in Loop C of the Fruita Campground. It starts to climb at a log fence 0.5 mile from the trailhead. The presence of much plant life, such as cottonwood trees and wild rose bushes, shows the influence of the river. Watch for signs of deer, marmot, and beaver.

When the trail leaves the river, it rises through different colors and textures of rock strata as it approaches the top of the

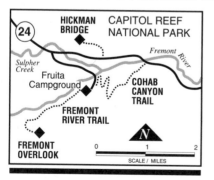

mesa. When pausing for breath, turn around and look back at the smooth domes of white Navajo sandstone that give Capitol Reef its name. They reminded early pioneers of the domes of capitol buildings. Near the top, look for spiky green leafless Mormon tea and silvery gray-green buffaloberry. Keep climbing.

The trail switches back around to the left and through a pinyon/ juniper forest to a large rock cairn marking the trail's end. A 360-degree vista of the Fruita Valley and Waterpocket Fold Escarpment rewards those who finish the hike.

Cohab Canyon Trail

1.25 miles, one-way, year-round

There are two ways to hike the Cohab Canyon Trail. One is to ascend the steep switchbacks across the road from the entrance to the Fruita Campground. On the way up, hikers may want to stop on the plentiful smooth, black boulders to rest. An outstanding view of the Fruita orchards, old barn, and "reef" sandstone formations from the top rewards those who make it to the canyon entrance.

At the top of the switchbacks, the cliffs are pocked with honeycomb-like holes. The trail seems to follow along the face of the tall cliff, when, surprisingly, the massive walls part and a side canyon opens up.

The trail turns to the left past house-size boulders. A steep-sided canyon with fantastically carved walls greets hikers. Look for jug-handled arches, windows, and plenty of child-size caves.

Walk along the sandy wash for 0.25 mile, looking for two-story-high elephant-shaped rocks. The wash eventually widens out and there is plenty of fine sand here for children to enjoy. Be sure to protect the plant and animal communities of the wash, taking special care not to walk on the crusty, black cryptobiotic soil near the trail.

The wash falls away into a dry slickrock waterfall. At this point, the trail is marked by cairns to the left and opens up into a large rock amphitheater, another potential playground. Climb on jungle-gym-size boulders, marvel at rock pillars, and listen to footsteps as they bounce off the steep surrounding walls.

Follow cairns down the lava boulder-lined trail. Walk in the same direction the water travels in rainstorms, over polished and sculpted stone in the sandy bottom. Here, trail markers present the option of a 3.5-mile trail (one-way) to Cassidy Arch across the Frying Pan Canyon area. The trail ends in the Grand Wash. Turn right and hike 0.25 mile to the Grand Wash parking area, where hikers can be picked up if prior arrangements have been made.

If you opt not to cross the Frying Pan, hike 0.75 mile farther across the mesa and descend gently to Highway 24 and the Hickman Bridge parking area. This is the other way to reach Cohab Canyon. Hikers should start from south of the Hickman Bridge parking area. Cross Highway 24 and over the Fremont River Bridge. The trailhead is on the right (south) side of the road. With less of an elevation gain, this is the easiest way to reach Cohab Canyon.

Groups with two drivers and several children can split up. Older kids can hike the switchbacks near the campground. Younger children can take the more gentle route from the bridge. Simply switch car keys as the two groups pass on the trail.

Cathedral Valley Trail

1.1 miles, one-way, March–November

Most of the fun involved with the remote Cathedral Valley hike is simply getting to the trailhead. Where most of the other major trailheads in Capitol Reef National Park are located on or near pavement, reaching this one requires a vehicle with high clearance, preferably four-wheel-drive, and a sense of adventure. The drive goes through a remote red-rock desert guarded by the monolithic buttes that give the valley its name.

Before driving to the trailhead, check on current road and weather conditions with rangers at the visitor center. Families with four-wheel-drive vehicles should have no trouble complet-

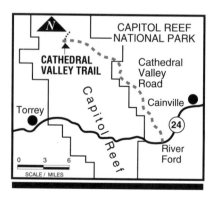

ing the loop. Those with two-wheel-drive can often enjoy the dirt road trip, via the Caineville Wash Road, but will not be able to complete the loop.

From the visitor center, drive east on Highway 24 out of the park, 18.6 miles to the Caineville Wash crossing. Then, look for a dirt road marked with a sign indicating

Cathedral Valley at Capitol Reef National Park

Cathedral Valley on the left (north) side of the highway. Follow this road about 26 miles to the well-marked trailhead. Families may want to take a side trip to rock formations called the Temple of the Moon and the Sun. There are places here to enjoy some rock scrambling and exploring off the beaten path.

The trailhead is located in Upper Cathedral Valley. The hike involves climbing up a trail for a few hundred yards to the top of a ridge in a pinyon/juniper forest full of yucca, buffaloberry, and Mormon tea. Pieces of petrified wood can be seen along the trail, but resist the temptation to take any. This is a national park so collecting anything is illegal. The hike ends at an overlook and comes close to the cliff edge at several locations. Watch children closely and make certain they stay on the trail. Two-wheel-drive vehicles should return the way they came and not attempt to complete the loop drive.

Goblin Valley State Park

Goblin Valley, a 3,654-acre preserve that features hundreds of mushroom-like rock formations of all shapes and sizes, is located between the southern Utah towns of Green River and Hanksville near the San Rafael Swell. Traveling west on Interstate 70 from Green River, take the Hanksville exit on Highway 24. Drive south toward Hanksville about 25 miles until a sign at the Temple Mountain junction directs you to Goblin Valley. Drive 14 miles southwest on paved and improved dirt roads to reach the park. Facilities include a 21-unit campground with modern restrooms that have hot water and showers, observation overlook, recreational-vehicle overlooks, and picnic tables. Campground reservations, which are suggested for April, May, June, September, and October weekends, are available through the Utah Division of Parks and Recreation. The nearest private accommodations are in Hanksville. Do not be afraid to explore canyons such as Wild Horse and Crack in the nearby San Rafael Swell. Ask a park ranger for directions to the Swell.

Goblin Valley brings out the "kid" in kids.

Though relatively small and off the beaten track, Goblin Valley ranks among the best kids' destinations in the Southwest. Though there are two developed hiking trails, the entire park resembles a giant red rock playground. Hundreds of soft sandstone "goblin" formations dot the valley. Through the erosion processes of wind and water, softer sediments are washed away, leaving mushroom-shaped goblins. There is nothing quite like visiting this place when a summer thunderstorm hits the area. All signs of humans are washed away as shallow chocolate-colored rivers reshape the goblins, only to quickly disappear into the soft soil. Most families simply let their children climb on top of the goblins, discover hidden nooks and crannies, or take time to give names to the different Smurf-like formations.

Carmel Canyon

1.5 miles, one-way, year-round

This trail begins in the northeast corner of the overlook parking area and descends into a series of small, narrow canyons guaranteed to make children feel as if they are wandering through a sort of giant red rock labyrinth. Rock cairns, most painted blue, lead hikers through this maze.

A 200-foot-high rock "goblin" guards the first slot canyon. Ask each child to name the formation. Younger children may need help stepping down a few steep parts of the trail early in the hike. They can easily be helped down by parents. Older kids will delight in rock scrambling.

After stepping out of the first canyon, the trail heads west into a wash. Then, as a formation aptly called "The Three Sisters" looms above, the canyon narrows to almost nothing. Take time to allow children to play on the rocks, hike on the soft sandy hills, or play in the fine sand.

Near the end of the hike, the canyon becomes extremely narrow. Adults can, with no difficulty, touch both sides of the canyon with their hands. At one point, taller folks will have to duck to keep from bumping their heads on an overhang.

The hike ends on the paved road leading to the Goblin Valley overlook. Families can either take the short walk on the road back to their cars or turn the trip into a loop hike by walking back toward the campground to the Curtis Bench trailhead.

Curtis Bench Trail

3 miles, one-way, year-round

This hike may seem slightly boring at first. It leads up a service road just south of the Goblin Valley campground and ends at the parking area overlooking the valley. This is an easy place to get disoriented, so follow the signs and blue rock cairns closely. The hike can also be started on the southern part of the parking lot. Some of its best features can be enjoyed from that point without taking the full trail.

Some "goblins" can be on the large side.

Adults who start the hike at the trailhead south of the campground may be impressed by views of the magnificent Henry Mountains to the south and the tan, buff, orange, and red rock formations to the west. Kids who endure the climb to the top of the plateau and the walk along the plateau will soon be rewarded.

The trail descends into a narrow canyon full of "unborn" goblins—formations that have not turned into the distinctive mushroom-shaped creatures seen in the rest of the park. It is a good thing the blue-painted rock cairns point the way because a number of side canyons—most of which look quite similar—lead away. This place feels like a maze. There are little alcoves where kids can hide and surprise their folks. It is easy to feel children's enthusiasm return as they discover this world of slot canyons, rocky creatures, and mazes.

Natural Bridges National Monument

Natural Bridges National Monument, established in 1908, is located 40 miles west of Blanding 4 miles off Utah Highway 95 in southeastern Utah. Families can spend a few brief moments enjoying views of three natural bridges from 9-mile, one-way Bridge View Drive. They also can take several hours hiking to one, two, or all three bridges. If looking for an all-day hike, they can walk along the canyon bottom where wildlife, Anasazi ruins, and ancient rock art can be seen from one bridge to the other. One short (0.6-mile round-trip) hike leads to an overlook of Horsecollar Ruin.

There is a small, primitive 13-unit campground located in the midst of a pretty pinyon forest near the visitor center. There are vault toilets at the campground and modern restrooms at the visitor center. Camping sites often fill by 2:00 or 3:00 P.M. from April through October. An overflow area can accommodate other campers, including those with large trailers or motorhomes that exceed the campground's 21-foot limit. Check at the visitor center for availability. Entrance fees are collected, except during the off-season.

Owachomo Natural Bridge is an easy hike for children.

Though open year-round, the monument sits at an elevation of 6,500 feet, meaning that snow can sometimes close trails. For a good introduction to desert plants, take the short nature walk near the visitor center. The visitor center features a brief slide show, information on the monument, and a small bookstore.

Ask your children if they know the difference between a natural bridge and an arch. A natural bridge is formed by streams wearing away at rock, creating a hole. Arches are formed by cracks in the rock that are enlarged in the same way as natural bridges. The continued percolation of water through the cracks and repetitious freezing and thawing slowly enlarge the cracks and form either an arch or a natural bridge.

Sipapu Bridge Trail

1.2 miles, round-trip, spring–fall,
winter depending on conditions

When driving west along Bridge View Drive, this is the first bridge travelers will encounter. At a height of 220 feet with a span

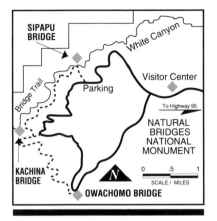

of 268 feet, a width of 31 feet, and a thickness of 53 feet, this is the world's second largest natural bridge. Only Rainbow Bridge, located on the banks of nearby Lake Powell, is larger. In the Hopi tradition, the word *sipapu* refers to an opening into the spirit world.

Families can look at the bridge from the overlook or hike to the bottom. The hike involves a 500-foot elevation change, climbing down two flights of stairs with handrails, and using three ladders to reach the bottom. It is the most difficult of the three hiking trails, but because kids love the sense of adventure of hiking into the steep canyon, it may also be the most exciting.

Though the bridge itself is spectacular, so is the hike. It seems to go straight down into the wash. The trail, except where the stairs descend, stays away from the edge of the cliffs. Kids will be tempted to get too close to the edge. Plan on close supervision if you take this trail.

Because of the fragile nature of the soil in this desert environment, stay on the trail if at all possible. Straying off can destroy black, crusty cryptobiotic soils, which prevent erosion and help plants take root.

Kachina Bridge Trail

0.8 mile, one-way, year-round,
spring–fall, winter depending on conditions

Kachinas play a central role in the Hopi tribe's religious traditions. Rock art found on this bridge resembles some of the symbols found on the Kachina dolls used in Hopi ceremonies.

Kachina Bridge, with its thickness of 93 feet, is the youngest of the three bridges in the monument. It has a height of 210 feet, a span of 204 feet, and a width of 44 feet, making it a massive rock formation.

A hike at Natural Bridges National Monument requires negotiating stairs.

Though Kachina Bridge can be seen from an overlook on Bridge View Drive, hikers who climb down 400 feet into a slickrock canyon so deep that handrails are required in certain spots are rewarded with two treats. First, there is the massive bridge itself. Take time to sit on a rock near the edge of this natural wonder and quietly contemplate its beauty. Children will enjoy playing in the sandy wash near its bottom. Second, during times of the year when water flows in the stream that created the bridge, a small waterfall flows through a hole in the rock in Armstrong Canyon a few hundred yards upstream from the bridge. Simply follow the wash where the waterfall—which can flow red after a rainstorm—has created a lush pool in Armstrong Canyon. Though this is a dry climate, the water in the stream has created a verdant garden at the bottom of the canyon.

Owachomo Bridge

*0.4 mile, round-trip, spring–fall,
winter depending on conditions*

The hike to this 180-foot-long bridge is the easiest in the monument. Though it, too, can be seen from an overlook near the road, the most inexperienced or youngest hiker should be able to finish the hike with a 180-foot elevation change. There are no stairs or ladders to negotiate on this gentle walk. Simply follow a winding rock path to the right of the overlook platform and walk underneath the formation.

The bridge gets its name from a Hopi word meaning "rock mound." Such a mound can be viewed on the east side of the bridge. A thin, narrow piece of rock, it is the oldest of the three monument bridges.

After a spring storm, tiny waterfalls appear almost magically under the white sandstone bridge. A natural amphitheater sits beneath the formation, providing a nice place to sit for awhile and appreciate the silence of the canyon. Armstrong Creek, which once flowed through the middle of the bridge and formed it, has changed its path and now can be seen below the formation.

Have your children look to the distant east where the aptly named Bears Ears Buttes can be seen in the midst of a pinyon/juniper forest.

Bryce Canyon National Park

Bryce Canyon is named after settler Ebeneezer Bryce, who came to the Paria Valley to live and harvest timber in 1875. The main entrance to the park is located 3 miles south of Utah Highway 12 on Utah Highway 63. Once in the park, that road winds along the rim of the Paunsaugunt Plateau for 18 miles, offering stops at 12 different overlooks. The Rim Trail stretches 5.5 miles and connects Fairyland and Bryce points. There are several hikes available in between these points along the road. The park visitor center, with a short informational slide program, small museum and bookstore, and park information, is located just south of the park entrance. It is open year-round except Thanksgiving, Christmas, and New Year's Day. During the summer months, when the park receives much of its visitation, other information can be obtained at the Sunrise Nature Center near the general store. Two campgrounds—North and Sunset—are open during the busy summer months. There are numerous private campgrounds outside the park and at nearby Dixie National Forest or at Kodachrome Basin or Escalante Petrified Forest state parks. One loop of the North Campground—with a heated, winterized restroom—stays open year-round.

Bryce can be an extremely cold winter destination with nighttime temperatures often dropping below zero. That should not discourage winter visits, however. Ruby's Inn, an historical commercial lodge located just outside the park entrance, grooms a number of cross-country ski trails leading to the park boundary. There is nothing quite like seeing fresh snow and blue skies contrasted with the almost fluorescent red and orange rocks that make up Bryce Canyon. The rim trail offers enjoyable ski experiences inside the park, which is often uncrowded in the winter months. The rim trail stretches 5.5 miles and connects Fairyland and Bryce points. The Park Service does not recommend skiing past Sunset Point on the Rim Trail. While Ruby's Inn and most motels outside the park boundary are open year-round, the

Hikers discovering a narrow Bryce Canyon passageway

Spires can be inspiring at Bryce Canyon National Park.

Bryce Canyon Lodge, restaurant, general store, showers, and laundry facilities remain open from April through October. That is when horseback and mule rides leading into the canyon are also offered. Because most of the hikes into Bryce Canyon require a steep climb, some families may opt to take a horseback ride.

The national park is an excellent place to enjoy midsummer wildflower displays. Botanists have identified over 400 different plant species. Birders have recognized more than 160 species. Young travelers enjoy participating in Bryce Canyon's Junior Ranger Program, offered during the summer months.

Navajo Loop

1.4 miles, one-way, year-round depending on snow depth

The Navajo Loop trail, with its 521-foot elevation change, begins at Sunset Point. It may be too steep for young children. At one point, hikers must negotiate a series of thirty switchbacks. However, the rewards for this work can be great because the walk leads through maze-like canyons and tunnels, offering in the process one of the most incredible hikes in the entire Four Corners region.

This is a cozy, protected walk that has the feel of creeping down the rabbit hole into a wonderland of unlikely shapes. This rabbit hole is not dark, however. It glows a brilliant orange ignited by the sun hitting its fluorescent walls and bouncing back and forth. Tall Douglas fir and ponderosa pine stand as sentinels along the way.

Children can find other metaphors to describe the scenery that stretches the imagination. They will certainly look up at the walls, often covered with dried, orange mud. This land of contrast, described by some as a fairyland, invites investigation.

Shortly after the first switchback, hikers can turn left or right. Though the choice is optional, parents can head right because the hiking trail is certain to immediately catch a child's attention. This part of the hike is known as Wall Street and with good reason. Like visiting the Wall Street area of New York City and being faced with towering skyscrapers, hikers entering Bryce's version find themselves in a narrow canyon flanked by steep orange walls. Children will instantaneously feel the majesty of Bryce.

There is also a practical reason for going right. The northern section of the loop—which features views of several of Bryce's more spectacular formations—involves the same amount of elevation gain but approaches the gain more gradually than the southern Wall Street portion of the trail. Either way, families need to realize "what goes up must come down" and expect a steep climb back to Sunset Point.

The middle of the loop levels out somewhat when hikers enter a towering ponderosa pine forest. A distinctive shrub, the greenleaf manzanita, covers the ground in places. Its bark is bright red, its leaves shiny green. This portion of the trail also allows a different perspective of Bryce because hikers look up at most of the formations instead of down on them from the rim.

Queen's Garden Trail

1.8 miles, one-way, year-round,
depending on snow depth

This hike with its 320-foot elevation change follows a slightly easier out-and-back hiking trail for families with young hikers who want to get a perspective of Bryce but want a little less elevation gain.

The trail begins at Sunrise Point and leads through a series of interesting rock formations that include Thor's Hammer, eventually leading to a pair of small natural bridges.

The Queen's Garden Trail encourages hikers to use their imaginations. Are the walls ahead natural, or could they be turrets of some huge castle, and are the rock "hoodoos" really disguised lookouts? Does this feel like walking through an underwater coral reef in which the sea has been drained away? Are the spires really a king's chess pieces?

Look for a hundred ways in which water has shaped this soft landscape. Geologists say the rim is actually eroding at the rate of 1 foot every 65 years.

Navajo Loop–Queen's Garden Combination

1.8 miles, round-trip, year-round,
ice or snow can close trail in winter

Families looking for a slightly longer Bryce Amphitheater hike—or an easier way of reaching the top after hiking through Wall Street on the Navajo Loop—might consider combining these two hikes. This will either involve a car shuttle from Sunset Point to Sunrise Point or one of the older family members walking an extra 0.5 mile along the paved rim trail that connects the two points.

The combination involves an elevation change of 521 feet and a distance of 2.9 miles. While it might be done in several ways, families can consider starting at Sunset Point and walking 0.6 mile down through Wall Street. The trail that connects the two hikes runs near the bottom of the amphitheater for 0.8 mile. When it reaches the Queen's Garden portion of the trek, hikers then must walk an additional 0.9 mile to the rim with a 320-foot elevation gain, making the walk out slightly easier.

Mossy Cave–Water Canyon

0.8 mile, round-trip, year-round,
ice and snow can close trail in winter

The trailhead for this easy walk begins near a bridge on Highway 12 between the turnoff to the park entrance and the tiny hamlet of Tropic. With only a 150-foot elevation change, this is a good hike for families with young children who want to enjoy some off-the-road scenery. Because it is not on the main canyon road,

Bryce Canyon offers hikers plenty of adventure.

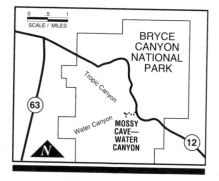

the hike typically is less crowded than those starting from the rim.

The reward at the end of this hike in early spring, late fall, and winter is a cave with frozen water formations that look like icy versions of some of the nearby rock spires in Bryce. In summer, seeping water creates a green hanging garden. Off to the right is a small waterfall.

National Park Service literature tells hikers to follow an historic irrigation ditch. After walking over two wooden foot bridges, hikers can go left to the cave or right to the waterfall.

Either way, the hike leads to some of the Four Corners region's most striking and unusual red rock scenery.

Kodachrome Basin State Park

Kodachrome Basin, named by a 1949 National Geographic Society expedition to southern Utah because of the many colors found in its rocks, features sixty-seven spires or chimneys. This is the world's largest concentration of such formations. Located 22 miles from Bryce Canyon National Park, this state park can be reached by driving east on Utah Highway 12 to the tiny hamlet of Cannonville. Follow the signs south 9 miles. The park features a horseback riding and stagecoach concession and a supply store that are open from April 1 through mid-October, a 27-unit campground, and modern restrooms with showers. Camping spots, cut from a pinyon/juniper forest, are spread far apart, making this an ideal spot for families with young children. Because the campground is becoming increasingly popular, reservations are suggested.

Kodachrome Basin State Park is a children's wonderland.

The park's six major hiking trails are all under 5 miles. With the possible exception of the 0.5-mile Eagles View Trail that involves a steep climb up the face of the Basin's north boundary, all are ideal for children. Trails include the 3-mile Panorama (with a 2-mile additional loop to an impressive box canyon called Cool Cave); the 0.5-mile Eagles View; the 1-mile Angels Palace; a 0.25-mile self-guided nature trail; the 1-mile Grand Parade Trail; and the 0.25-mile Shakespeare Arch walk. By driving an additional 10 miles south of the park entrance on a dirt road, visitors can also see Grosvenor Arch, an impressive buff-colored double arch located on Bureau of Land Management property.

Angels Palace Trail

1 mile, round-trip, year-round

Though short, the Angels Palace Trail contributes plenty of interest to stir young imaginations. Part of the fun of Kodachrome

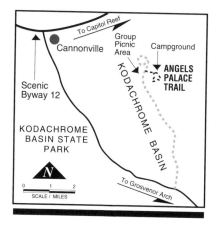

Basin is asking children to name the rocks. Formations resemble dinosaurs, Fred Flintstone, geysers, buffalos, and bears. The trail begins across the road from the group picnic area near the campground entrance. After crossing a wash, hikers enter a narrow canyon almost immediately.

After a short walk through the canyon, the trail gradually climbs up the side of a red hill. At the top, good rock-scrambling opportunities in unusual rock formations reward hikers. So do views of the surrounding pinyon juniper-covered plateaus. This is a good spot to look down on some of the park's famous spires, giving visitors a good overall view of the basin.

Escalante State Park

Located 44 miles east of Bryce Canyon on Highway 12, 1 mile west of the town of Escalante, this small state park contains a surprising number of things to do. Its 22-unit campground features covered picnic tables, a nice grassy area where families can throw Frisbees or play football, and restrooms with hot showers. Reservations are suggested on most holiday weekends. The campground is located within walking distance of Wide Hollow Reservoir, which features boating, swimming, and fishing for trout, bass, and bluegill. Designated a Utah watchable wildlife area, the reservoir also hosts migrating ducks, shorebirds, bald eagles, and osprey much of the year.

This is also an excellent base camp from which to explore the Escalante Canyon area. Go to the nearby Escalante multi-agency contact station and ask about visiting the Bureau of Land Management's nearby Devils Garden and Calf Creek Falls recreation areas or the U.S. Forest Service's Boulder Mountain area.

A 1-mile self-guided hiking trail (with an optional 0.75-mile loop) leads to a petrified wood forest. In a cove near the park's group area, tons of specimens have been imported so that those not wishing to take the hike can still view petrified wood.

Petrified Forest– Trail of Sleeping Rainbows

1-mile nature trail, loop, year-round;
0.75 mile, loop, year-round

This short but interesting self-guided nature trail begins north of the park visitor center and quickly climbs to a plateau that overlooks the campground and Wide Hollow Reservoir. Numbered posts help young hikers discover this high desert world of balanced

Devils Garden is near the town of Escalante.

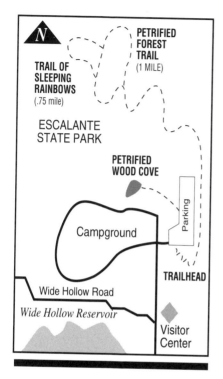

rocks, desert varnish, pygmy forests, and painted deserts. Adults will likely be impressed with the views.

Unfortunately, many past visitors violated park regulations by picking up and keeping much of the petrified wood along the main trail. Encourage children to avoid the temptation of keeping even a small piece, as collecting is prohibited in the park so that others may have something to enjoy.

Because much of the petrified wood on the main trail is gone, the best petrified wood examples—and there are some incredibly large and colorful pieces to see in the early parts of the trail—can be viewed on the appropriately named Trail of Sleeping Rainbows. This 0.75-mile loop involves a very steep descent and then ascent back to the main trail. Because hikers view a forest of 150-million-year-old trees, it is well worth the effort. Young hikers intimidated by the climb need walk only the first block to see fine examples of petrified wood.

Anasazi Indian Village State Park

This state park, which interprets the history of the Kayenta Anasazi who lived on the site from 1050 to 1200, is located on Highway 12, 78 miles east of Bryce Canyon in the small community of

Boulder. Eighty-seven rooms on the site, only 20 of which are open for viewing, were excavated by the University of Utah in 1958 and 1959. No camping is available on the site itself, but U.S. Forest Service facilities on nearby Boulder Mountain and the Bureau of Land Management's popular Calf Creek Recreation Area are located within a few miles of the museum. The park is a good place to ask for information on hiking and driving possibilities in the area. The picnic area is a shaded respite for visitors traveling between Bryce Canyon and Capitol Reef national parks. An auditorium, museum, and gift shop interpret the Anasazi culture.

Anasazi Self-Guided Trail

100 yards, one-way, year-round

Children need to walk only 100 yards to learn about what life was like for the Anasazi 1,000 years ago. Easy-to-read signs offer information on the daily life and rituals of these ancient people. Kids especially enjoy crawling through a life-size, six-room replica of an Anasazi dwelling or grinding corn on a rock mano and metate the way the "Ancient Ones" performed the task hundreds of years ago.

Moab

Once a uranium town struggling for its existence when mining the yellow mineral became unprofitable, Moab now mines for tourist dollars. Though children oftentimes enjoy taking a stroll through the Hollywood Stuntman's Hall of Fame Museum in town, Moab's real value to tourists is its location. Situated in the heart of southeastern Utah, this town of about 5,000 residents is a hub for tourism. With hundreds of hotel rooms, several large recreational-vehicle parks, a huge supermarket, many interesting restaurants, and tourist-oriented shops, it is a place many visitors stay while exploring the surrounding Canyonlands Country.

Since Moab is located on the banks of the Colorado River, it has become the headquarters for a number of river-rafting companies. Families looking for whitewater adventure may want to try a two-day trip through Westwater Canyon or a four- or five-day adventure down Cataract Canyon. Day river trips are also popular. There are also jet-boat trips, flatwater canoeing, and a night-time boat tour of Canyonlands. Outfitters also rent four-wheel-drive vehicles to allow families to explore the old backcountry roads found in Arches and Canyonlands national parks as well as adjacent Bureau of Land Management property. There are a number of dispersed or lightly developed BLM campgrounds along the Colorado River. The nearby La Sal Mountains, part of the Manti–La Sal National Forest, also offer camping, hiking, touring, and wildlife viewing opportunities as well as good cross-country skiing in the winter. .

Nothing has fueled Moab's tourist economy in recent years quite like mountain biking, however. The famed Slickrock Bicycle Trail, located just outside the city limits, takes mountain bikers over petrified sand dunes. Not for the faint of heart or the out-of-shape, a 2-mile practice loop and a longer tour along the edge of a canyon overlooking the Colorado River lead bikers on a wild ride. This trail is appropriate for young children to walk on but definitely not to bicycle. There are easier trails in the Moab area. A number of bicycle rental shops in town also offer guided tours. If unfamiliar with the area, that is the best way to go.

Those looking for detailed information can visit a travel center in the middle of town that is jointly operated by state and federal land management agencies and the Grand County Travel Council. Detailed maps, advice on availability of campsites, and detailed information on the Four Corners area can be found here in what is one of the better information centers in the Southwest.

Canyonlands National Park

Canyonlands has a reputation for being one of the wilder and more remote parks in the national park system. In the case of two of its four districts—the Maze and Rivers—that is true. With the

Hiking at Canyonlands National Park

exception of a small corner—Horseshoe Canyon—the Maze can be reached by four-wheel-drive, foot, or mountain bike. The Island in the Sky and Needles districts, however, are easily accessible by two-wheel-drive cars.

The Green and Colorado rivers can be enjoyed on a rafting trip or by taking a long hike or mountain-biking trip to the edge of the rivers. The upper stretches of both rivers are home to great canoeing. Family rafting or canoeing trips are possible with jet boats available commercially to pick travelers up at the confluence of the Green and Colorado.

The Island in the Sky District on the north end of the park and the Needles District on the south provide visitors with paved access roads and both difficult and easy hikes. The Needles is located southwest of Moab on paved Utah Highway 211 west of US 191. Though Highway 211 dead ends at a difficult four-wheel-drive road, the Needles serves visitors with a good visitor center and the park's best camping facility.

Since the Squaw Flat Campground often fills early in the day from March through the end of October, campers should plan on being flexible when visiting the Needles District. The commercial Needles Outpost just outside the park has showers, a small store, and camping. The nearby Abajo (Blue) Mountains, on U.S. Forest Service property, contain some campgrounds and fishing lakes at a slightly higher elevation. The Island in the Sky District west of Moab has a paved loop road, which also dead ends, and a more primitive and smaller campground.

Dead Horse State Park, located near the Canyonlands boundary, has modern restrooms (no showers) and a campground where reservations can be made through the state park system. Park headquarters, lodging, grocery stores, and commercial rafting, mountain biking, and four-wheel-drive tours can be found in Moab, Monticello, and other nearby communities.

Park rangers urge hikers to stay on the trails. Parents should be especially careful to point out the delicate, black, crustlike cryptobiotic soil on top of the red sand. This crust helps prevent erosion and forms a soil crust where plants can grow.

The Needles Roadside Ruin

0.25 mile, one-way, year-round

Perhaps the easiest of all Canyonlands hikes, this 0.25-mile loop trail begins just south of the Needles Visitor Center. It intro-

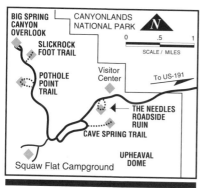

duces the natural history of the park through the use of a self-guided trail brochure. The brochure introduces the desert plant species that occupy this high, red rock desert.

Children can walk across hardened sandstone called slickrock, darting from rock cairn to rock cairn. Learning to follow these cairns—basically just piles of rocks along the slickrock—is a useful skill to learn in both Canyonlands and other Four Corners parks.

What is more, at the halfway point in the trail children can view a small, ancient Anasazi granary hidden under a little alcove. Since it is not obvious until hikers come up next to it, have kids search for it. The door of the structure is on top. It is illegal to climb up to or on the granary, which is believed to have been constructed around A.D. 950.

Cave Spring Trail

0.6 mile, loop, year-round

What kid—or adult for that matter—can resist ducking under alcoves, searching for ancient rock writings and learning the history of old cowboys? This loop trail offers much adventure in a short but exciting hike. In fact, parents who do not like watching their kids climb up ladders or duck under alcoves may not enjoy this walk.

To reach the trailhead, drive west of the Needles visitor center. Take the road toward Salt Creek. Then, instead of heading south to Salt Creek (this turns into a difficult four-wheel-drive road), drive east about 1 mile on the dirt road.

The first destination is a cowboy line camp. Though once located at a spring that will be seen a little farther up the trail, this camp under an alcove allows hikers to view the stove, horse tack, chair, table, and camping gear used by the cowboys of the late 1800s who ran cattle in this area. A self-guided trail brochure can prove useful to interpret some of this history.

The trail leads under other alcoves. Look for ancient Anasazi rock writing along the way at the backs of some of the alcoves. Signs identify trees and shrubs. At one point, hikers come to a spring with a beautiful desert garden. On hot summer days, the shade of the alcove coupled with the cooling effect of water make this one of the few hikes children can enjoy in the middle of the day. In fact, in all of the Four Corners area, it is a good idea to begin hikes early or late in the day, leaving the hot midafternoon for naps or visits to museums.

Cave Spring Trail hikers eventually must climb an eleven-step wooden ladder and a seven-step wooden ladder to reach the top of the mesa where they can enjoy views of the distant La Sal and

Abajo mountains as well as the sharp, narrow pinnacles that give the Needles District its name. The trail meanders fairly close to the edge of the little canyon. Watch children closely, and make sure to follow the cairns. Once on top of the slickrock, it is easy to wander off the trail.

Pothole Point

0.6 mile, loop, year-round

National Park Service rangers tell hikers that potholes are depressions in the slickrock that hold water after rainstorms. They also contain their own life systems and should be left undisturbed. That is why park rangers ask hikers not to play, wade, or swim in the potholes.

By following this trail and using the self-guided brochure, parents can introduce their children to the world of potholes and enjoy views of Canyonlands country in the process. The trail starts near the end of the pavement on the road to the Big Spring Canyon Overlook. There are literally dozens of little potholes along the way.

Children dancing along the slickrock at Canyonlands National Park

As hikers read the trail guide while walking the scenic trail, they will learn that potholes, once started, continue to grow. They become traps for windblown sand grains and pebbles, often collecting rainwater that serves wildlife well in the dry desert environment. Collected rainwater also helps break down the "cement" that holds the sandstone slickrock together. Tiny creatures such as four different species of shrimp can lie dormant for years, only to hatch and thrive when rains fill potholes with water and the temperature is neither too hot nor too cold.

As hikers walk around a large, gnarly sandstone formation in the middle of the trail, they can survey the surrounding area.

Island in the Sky Mesa Arch

0.5 mile, loop, year-round

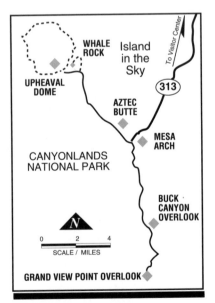

Though this alluring trail is easy, it is also somewhat dangerous. Parents should not allow their children to run ahead because this wonderful arch formed in Navajo sandstone sits on the edge of a 400-foot dropoff.

The loop trail begins 6 miles south of the Island in the Sky Visitor Center. Pick up a trail brochure to learn along the way about natural features such as cryptobiotic soil, blackbrush, pinyon pine, Utah juniper, Mormon tea, narrowleaf yucca, prickly pear cactus, mountain mahogany, and single-leaf ash.

The view of the La Sal Mountains through the middle of the arch, especially in winter, makes for a wonderful photograph.

The Island in the Sky district offers panoramic views.

Upheaval Dome

0.5 mile, one-way, to 8 miles (optional),
loop, year-round

This trail leads from a picnic area at the northern end of one of the two paved spur roads in Island in the Sky. Hikers have several choices when seeking a chance to see this mysterious depression in the ground. There are two overlooks. The closest involves a 0.5-mile hike (one-way) with a 200-foot uphill elevation gain. Another overlook can be reached by hiking 1 mile (one-way) with a 500-foot elevation. Families with older children looking for a day hike can take a loop trail around the dome that is 8 miles long and involves a 1,300-foot elevation change. It is possible to walk from the overlook partway on the loop trail and then return without doing the full 8-mile loop.

The trails offer views of a crater-like geologic formation. Geologists, frankly, are not certain what caused the dome to form. Before offering the various theories to your children, ask them what they think formed the hole before them.

Some geologists think the impact of a meteor formed the

crater-like formation. Others figure it is the result of a deep layer of salt that, according to the National Park Service, squished up, bending and pushing the layers of rock above it. Scientific tests have been undertaken to determine its geologic origin and results will be released in the future.

Whichever theory hikers buy, the formation does give them a geology lesson. Use a trip to the visitor center for an introduction to the different rocks in the area and then attempt to tell the difference between the Navajo, Kayenta, Wingate, Chinle, Moenkopi, and White Rim sandstones that are exposed here.

Whale Rock

0.75 mile, one-way, year-round

Located just east of Upheaval Dome, Whale Rock does, indeed, look like a giant whale from a Walt Disney animated movie. As you drive toward the trailhead, ask children if they can discover the whale in the desert.

Though climbing to the top of the whale's back involves some rock scrambling up slickrock, most kids will enjoy the scramble. The short hike leads to the top of the rock, with views of the Upheaval Dome rim and the La Sal Mountains of the surrounding areas.

Children climbing on Whale Rock

Grand View Point

1 mile, one-way, year-round

Grand View Point is reached by taking the southern paved road to its end. It can be seen in a few seconds or by walking along the rim.

Most children are not impressed with grand views. They tend to look for either hiking challenges or small entertainments in front of them. But even kids who do not like views will likely be impressed with the views here. Ask if they can identify the Chocolate Drops that can be seen to the west in the distant Maze District. On a clear day, the three major mountain ranges in southwestern Utah—the La Sals, Abajos, and Henrys—can be enjoyed from this point.

Once again, there are steep dropoffs here. Take care to watch your children closely.

Arches National Park

Located 5 miles north of Moab, this small national park ranks among the most popular family vacation destinations in the Four Corners area largely because most of its trails are short, accessible, and easy walks. The 18-mile drive from the park entrance near US 191 to the point where the road dead ends at Devils Garden and the campground allows views of balanced rocks, natural arches, and red-colored rock formations. Ask children to come up with their own names for the odd-shaped red rocks while driving from point to point. As its name implies, the park features more than 200 natural arches formed in Entrada sandstone by erosional forces and time. Because of its relatively small size, Arches can become crowded. Its 53-unit campground fills early in the day from March through November. Do not be surprised if you have to camp at nearby Dead Horse Point or Green River state park—where advance reservations can be made—or at any of a number of privately owned campgrounds in the area. There are no commercial facilities of any kind inside the park, but lodging, food, and gas can be found in nearby Moab. Because of summer's scorching heat and heavy visitation, fall and spring may be the best times to visit. After a wet winter, spring desert wildflower displays cover the red, sandy desert around the park. In winter, snow-covered red rocks and the high La Sal Mountains contrast strikingly with clear, blue skies.

The park schedules a number of fine interpretive programs. Families lucky enough to get a campsite in the midst of the junipers and fine pink sand should not miss the campfire programs, largely because the amphitheater is framed by Skyline Arch. Also, get reservations for a ranger-guided tour of the maze-like Fiery Furnace. Once inside this land of tall sandstone fins and narrow box canyons, it is easy to become disoriented. This, of course, creates a sense of adventure that most rangers use to make this one of the more interesting guided hikes a family will ever take. The visitor center—with its adjacent self-guided trail providing a guide to Arches' plant life—is located near the park entrance, offering restrooms, water, a small museum, an introductory slide show, and books for sale.

One last note: Because of the fragile nature of cryptobiotic soil—the black, crust-like substance essential to preventing erosion and giving plants a place to grow in the desert environment—stay on the trails.

Delicate Arch

3 miles, round-trip, year-round

This classic hike across a wash, up a slickrock trail, and along the edge of a canyon can be deceivingly difficult, especially in the middle of a hot summer afternoon when the 480-foot elevation gain seems much more severe. But the reward at the end more than makes up for the effort.

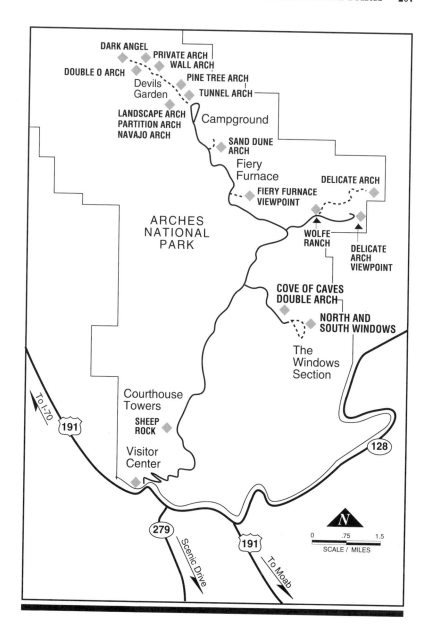

A hike to Delicate Arch is an unforgettable experience.

Expect to share the trail except early in the morning or late in the evening. In fact, the parking lot often fills on busy summer days as a steady stream of hikers trudges up the trail. When the parking lot fills, the Park Service does not allow overflow parking.

The trek starts at the Wolfe Ranch, built by Civil War veteran John Wesley Wolfe in 1888 on the banks of the Salt Wash. Before using the swinging bridge to walk across the wash, take a few minutes to read the interpretive signs and learn about the difficult life of a rancher. Tour the cabin, corral, and root cellar before walking across the swinging bridge and beginning a climb up to the next level of sandstone.

Hikers soon find themselves walking from rock cairn to rock cairn across the brilliant red slickrock, following the well-worn trail of the thousands who made the trip before them. The path leads to the edge of a canyon and is cut out of sandstone. Parents will want to watch their children closely at this point because there are a few steep dropoffs. When a small arch appears high on the right in the sandstone wall, it is a sign that the ultimate destination of this hike is getting closer. Curiosity builds because, unlike some of the other hikes at Arches, hikers do not see Delicate Arch until the last possible second. Most do not forget their first view of this wondrous 46-foot-high rock formation with its 32-foot opening. Perched on the edge of a natural sandstone amphitheater, the formation seems like an impossible quirk of nature. Many people like to hike under the arch to have their photographs taken, but this is not advisable for families with young children. The dropoff on the south side of the arch is steep and dangerous.

Sand Dune Arch

0.2 mile, one-way, year-round

Located on the west side of the road near the north end of the paved park road, this easy walk is a "don't miss" attraction for parents traveling with young hikers under the age of five. Do not let the short distance be deceptive. Most youngsters become so enchanted with this place that it is not unusual to spend the better part of a morning or afternoon enjoying it. Letting young toddlers walk into this place can be the highlight of a family trip.

The trail heads off from the parking lot across a flat, open area and leads into a narrow slot canyon. To some, the entrance resembles something out of a Dr. Seuss story as children peer into the dark, narrow crack. Adults can touch both sides of the canyon in spots.

Sand Dune Arch, a small but impressive rock formation, is hidden inside this narrow, shady canyon. Like its name suggests, a dune of fine pink sand is located underneath the rock formation. Kids delight in climbing up the dune, rolling down it, and burying hands and feet in the cool sand. Toddlers spend hours in this special place inventing new games and enjoying a natural playground.

The Windows

0.9 mile, round-trip, year-round;
Double Arch, 0.25 mile, one-way, year-round

Right before turning off the 2.5-mile-long entrance road to the Windows section of Arches approximately 9 miles from the park entrance, visitors are greeted with a most incredible sight: A balanced rock—looking more improbable than anything seen at a Disney theme park—sits precariously on top of a rock pillar. First-time visitors often stop to walk around the rock, take a photo, and

Along the trail at Arches National Park

simply study the implausible sight of a huge rock balanced on the top of a narrower pillar.

Driving west into the Windows section, families can view a number of large arches from their automobiles. Better yet, they can take short hikes to enjoy a closer look.

Most families, at one time or another, view the movie "Indiana Jones and the Last Crusade." That is why Double Arch, one of the dominant features of the drive through the Windows section of the park, will look so familiar. It served as a natural "prop" for an early scene in the movie when a young Indiana Jones discovered a treasure in a fictional cave at its base.

The bounty most families will take with them after taking the short and easy 0.25-mile hike to the base of the massive Double Arch is a vacation memory. At sunset, on an autumn evening, the wind sometimes whistles through the box canyon at the end of the trail, sending the fine sand particles that scoured out this impressive formation flying. Those lucky enough to visit the place during a rare rainstorm can watch waterfalls appear like magic, only to disappear into the fine sand.

A hike of just under 1 mile (round-trip) leads to North and South Window and Turret Arch. Young hikers enjoy stopping and counting the number of arches they can see from this one place.

Devils Garden

2 miles, one-way, year-round

Devils Garden, located on the loop where the road circles around and begins its return to the visitor center, offers families many choices. It is a fascinating place of high red rock walls, hidden canyons, and intriguing arches with a number of side trails. Spend an hour taking the 0.3-mile walk to Tunnel Arch or the 0.4-mile trek to Pine Tree Arch. Take several hours to walk the 2 miles to Double O Arch and nearby Private Arch, which a hiker discovered just a few years ago.

The trail leads through a desert rock garden to eight major arches and many other small windows. Arches include Tunnel, Pine Tree, Landscape, Wall, Partition, Navajo, Private, and Double O. From Double O, a rock pinnacle known as the Dark Angel can be viewed in the distance. Landscape Arch may be the most popular destination, largely because its 306-foot span is one of the longest known spans in the world.

From Double O Arch, an impressive formation with "O"-shaped arches stacked on top of one another, hikers can explore Private Arch and then take a longer (about 2 miles) walk through Fin Canyon where several large arches can be enjoyed. These trails are not quite as well developed but can be followed, creating a loop hike where more of the park can be seen.

Because the elevation gains are not difficult and shady spots can be found along the trail, the Devils Garden area is an ideal place for families to experiment with longer hikes. This is especially true if they are lucky enough to be staying in the nearby Devils Garden campground.

Corona Arch

1.5 miles, one-way, year-round

Though located near Arches National Park, Corona Arch is found on Bureau of Land Management property. To reach the trailhead for this interesting—and often uncrowded—3-mile round-trip hike, drive north from Moab across the Colorado River bridge on US 191. Turn down Scenic Byway 279 on the north side of the Colorado River. Along the way, road signs point out ancient Native American rock writing panels as well as a place to view dinosaur tracks. The viewpoints are worth a quick look. A sign that reads "Corona Arch, Bow Tie Arch" directs hikers to a parking lot across the Colorado River.

Hikers will cross some railroad tracks near the trailhead and then slowly work their way up some switchbacks. Before the trail begins turning into a wide canyon, stop and look back at some nice views of the Colorado River below. Kids can experiment with echoes as they enter the canyon. Try a quick shout at about the point the trail turns from sand and gravel to slickrock.

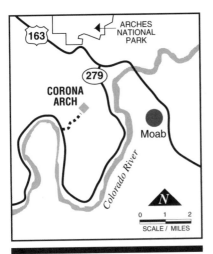

Corona Arch—with its 140-foot-by-105-foot opening (someone once flew a small airplane through it!)—can be viewed from a distance. But walking underneath this and nearby Bow Tie Arch allows the most impressive views.

To reach these views, hikers use a primitive chain railing that trail builders cemented into the rock to help boost them up a steep portion of the trail. A few feet farther, hikers climb a ladder. Though not especially dangerous, the

Children are impressed by gigantic Corona Arch.

chains and ladder will give children a sense of adventure, adding to the fun of the walk. Stop for a few moments at the small alcove at the top of this trail. The acoustics are such that footsteps and voices from Corona Arch—still a good distance away—can be heard. To test the sound while hiking with several people, leave a few under the alcove and let the others hike to the arch.

Do not miss the hanging garden that adds touches of green and black to the surrounding red rock. The garden is located under Bow Tie Arch, which seems to be a natural conduit for water flowing above.

Walk to the base of Corona Arch where the sheer size of the natural formation seems certain to create a lasting family memory.

Hovenweep National Monument

One of the least visited of all the national monuments in the Four Corners region, Hovenweep consists of six groups of ruins. These include the Square Tower Ruins—the best and most well preserved in the monument—and the Cajon in Utah and the Holly, Hackberry Canyon, Cutthroat Castle, and Goodman Point Ruins in Colorado. All are reached via dirt roads, which are passable by passenger car except in rare cases of bad weather. A small ranger station–museum–visitor center located at the edge of the Square Tower Ruins complex serves as park headquarters. A 31-unit campground with flush toilets and running water is located in the monument.

The Square Tower Ruins and Campground are most easily reached by driving on US 163 south through Blanding and taking the turnoff east to the Hatch Trading Post. There, drive east 16 miles on a dirt road to the visitor station. There are no commercial services inside the monument, so pick up supplies at the Hatch Trading Post or at the Ismay Trading Post 14 miles to the southeast.

Square Tower Loop Trail

2 miles, loop, year-round if road to park is passable

The silence of the desert greets visitors to this trail, which leads to the famous Square Tower ruin. The 2-mile Square Tower Trail includes views of a large number of ruins in a relatively short distance on a trail that most families will have little trouble negotiating. A trail brochure is available at the visitor center.

The dwellings are built on top and below the cliff that surrounds a small desert canyon. One is found under an alcove. The loop trail winds around both sides of the canyon so front and rear views of the ruins can be seen. In order to preserve the ruins and protect unexcavated rubble at the base of some of the ruins, the

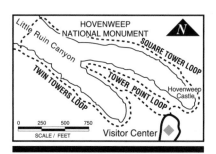

trail stays, for the most part, on the slickrock canyon rim, not far from the edge. It is level, except for a short, steep turn down to the canyon bottom and up the other side. The trail starts at the visitor center parking lot next to some picnic tables.

The first stop is Hovenweep

Castle. It has walls so well built that, even with the mortar used to hold them together long gone, the quality of the construction is obvious. This ruin, along with others in the area, was built with no ground-level doors, except on the steep canyon side. It was built in the 1200s, about the same time castles were being constructed in Europe. Far up on its walls are tiny square holes. They provide views of the land in all directions. Archaeologists have also discovered that these holes have astronomical significance. They seem to have indicated certain important dates to the ancient farmers who once worked the land here, especially at the beginning of summer and winter.

Past Hovenweep Castle, look back up to the head of the canyon and other ruins at the bottom. Some are nestled far back under the alcove.

Farther up the trail, as soon as a square tower is seen on one side of the canyon and a round tower on another, look for other ruins. These cliff dwellings are just the upper story to pueblos that started on the canyon bottom but are now in ruins. Examine the excellent masonry of the Twin Towers. It was done in the Mesa Verde style like the other pueblos found in this area of the Southwest.

From Twin Towers, hikers can stroll 0.5 mile back to their vehicles near the visitor center. Or they can elect to continue the trail to Twin Towers Loop. Soon, the trail turns abruptly left down the canyon. The way is marked by rock cairns. Both down and back involve a short but steep walk. As hikers walk along this side of the canyon, they can view the front side of the dwellings across the canyon and the rear of dwellings on this side of the canyon. A pair of binoculars will enhance the hike. A trail takes off to the right for those going directly to the campground from here.

Next stop is Stronghold House. Its only evident entrance could be reached by hand-and-toe holds in the canyon wall. While at Stronghold House, search the wall for additional dwellings. Do not miss the dwellings partially remaining in the recesses of a giant boulder.

The trail forks not far from here to the left and follows the old Twin Towers Loop northwest for a while and then returns to the visitor center. Hikers can cut their walk short and take a marked side trail back to their vehicles.

Edge of the Cedars State Park

Though small in comparison with other ruins complexes in the Four Corners region, Edge of the Cedars State Park on the outskirts of the southeastern Utah town of Blanding delivers a large amount of history on ancient peoples and more modern settlers. Because of some of the hands-on exhibits in its museum, it makes for a good family stop in the midst of a long drive. The museum, which is located next to a pre-Columbian ruin, is a self-guided experience. Displays present information not only on the area's ancient inhabitants but also on contemporary Navajo and Ute tribes and the Anglo settlers of San Juan County. Take note of the following exhibits in the museum: the Anasazi pottery collection; the Fragile Heritage Exhibit—unique Anasazi artifacts; the Spirit Windows Exhibit—Native American rock art; visible storage—a room into which the visitor can see the artifacts in storage; Special Exhibits Room—features art, photographic works, and video presentations. Visitors can climb to an observation tower and on a clear day enjoy views such as Shiprock in New Mexico, Ute Mountain in Colorado, the Carrizo Mountains in Arizona, and the Bears Ears in Utah. Four traditional Navajo sun shades cover picnic tables. The front of the museum features a botanical garden with a variety of native plants. An Indian garden of squash and corn is planted and maintained each growing season. The crops are planted in the traditional Native American way.

There is no camping on site. Developed campgrounds are located in the nearby Abajo Mountains or at Natural Bridges National Monument.

Ruins Walk

0.25 mile, loop, year-round

Though only 0.25-mile long, this self-guiding trail includes some interesting experiences for children. In using a guide to follow a series of numbered posts, hikers are introduced to the ancient people who once inhabited this area. It is not unusual to see archaeologists actually working on the site.

Hikers learn about kivas, the ceremonial chambers used by the ancient people. At one point, hikers are invited to climb down the ladder through a hole in the top of a roof of a restored kiva and to crawl inside, where they can sense what living in this complex may have been like. Storage rooms, living areas, and views of Westwater Canyon, Elk Ridge, and the massive Abajo (Blue) Mountains can also be enjoyed along the way.

Along the way, visitors can enter a Navajo hogan (a traditional Navajo house), still utilized by Navajos in the area.

Dinosaur National Monument

Located 20 miles east of Vernal on the Utah-Colorado border, Dinosaur National Monument may be north of most of the Four Corners attractions, but it is a must-see for younger children who almost always become fascinated with dinosaurs. Coupled with a visit to the state-operated Field House of Natural History in Vernal where lifelike dinosaurs are placed in an outdoor garden, most children—and their parents—will enjoy a trip to this national monument. The main attraction is the covered Dinosaur Quarry Visitor Center, located 7 miles north of US 40 and the Utah town of Jensen. The visitor center is a working center for paleontology. National Park Service technicians at one time could be seen working on exposing the fossilized bones under a covered roof as part of the visitor center. That has stopped for the time being, but visitors can view 1,600 dinosaur bones as they were deposited in the Morrison Formation. Stops at the visitor center include an overview from an observation deck, a closer look at the fossils and the rock that surrounds them, and a peek at the monument's laboratory. While dinosaurs are the big draw at the monument, there are many other outdoor activities available. These include short nature trails at Split Mountain, Lodore, and along the Harpers

Corner Road as well as a few longer trails. Commercial river outfitters offer day-long and multiple-day trips down the Yampa and Green rivers inside the park. The Split Mountain and Green River campgrounds near the quarry provide national park-style camping opportunities. More primitive camping experiences are available at Rainbow Park, Echo Park, Deerlodge Park, and Lodore. Families who enjoy driving for pleasure can take the 22-mile Cub Creek Scenic Drive after visiting the Quarry, taking time to visit the Josie Bassett Morris Cabin, view Indian rock art, or take some short trails along the way.

Sounds of Silence Route

2 miles, round-trip, year-round

Looking for an adventure in Dinosaurland? Seeking silence in solitude? Then this route, which begins at a well-marked trailhead about 1 mile from the Quarry visitor center entrance station on the north side of the road, is worth checking out.

The route is set up as a challenge because it is not marked like most National Park Service trails. Instead, it encourages children to explore the muddy canyons and slickrock areas and to complete the loop trail on their own. At times, families will need to count paces to make certain they are heading in the right direction. At others, children may get frustrated and think they are totally lost, only to find a place where the route picks up again. Obviously, younger hikers will need close adult supervision on this hike. Especially in the summer months, a good supply of water is recommended for each hiker.

The reason the walk is called Sounds of Silence is that it leads away from roads and into small canyons where the sounds of civilization are blocked out. This is a good place to encourage children to write or draw in a journal, contemplating the beauty and silence that surrounds them. At some points, the walk offers gratifying views of the Green River. At others, children can enjoy scrambling along slickrock.

Because of the way the route is put together, chances are families will feel lost at times, only to be excited again as they rediscover the route.

Appendix

IMPORTANT ADDRESSES

State Tourist Offices, National Parks and Monuments, U.S. Forest Service Offices, Bureau of Land Management Offices, Indian Reservations, State Parks, Nature Centers, and Wildlife Refuges

Arizona

Arizona Office of Tourism
1100 West Washington
Phoenix, Arizona 85007

Peaks Ranger Station
Coconino National Forest
5079 N. Highway 89
Flagstaff, Arizona 86004

Grand Canyon National Park
Grand Canyon, Arizona 86023

Petrified Forest National Park
Petrified National Forest,
    Arizona 86028

Sunset Crater Volcano
    National Monument
Route 3, Box 149
Flagstaff, Arizona 86004

Wupatki National Monument
P.O. Box 444A
Flagstaff, Arizona 86001

Canyon de Chelly
    National Monument
P.O. Box 588
Chinle, Arizona 86503

Glen Canyon National
    Recreation Area
P.O. Box 1507
Page, Arizona 86040

Montezuma Castle
    National Monument
P.O. Box 219
Camp Verde, Arizona 86332

Sedona Ranger District
Coconino National Forest
P.O. Box 300
Sedona, Arizona 86336

Walnut Canyon
    National Monument
Walnut Canyon Road
Flagstaff, Arizona 86004

Colorado

Alamosa/Monte Vista National
    Wildlife Refuge Complex
9383 El Rancho Lane
Alamosa, Colorado 81101

Anasazi Heritage Center
27501 Highway 184
Dolores, Colorado 81323

Black Canyon of the Gunnison
    National Monument
Box 1648
Montrose, Colorado 81401

Colorado National Monument
Fruita, Colorado 81521

Curecanti National
    Recreation Area
102 Elk Creek
Gunnison, Colorado 81230

Colorado Tourism Board
Eagle Direct
5105 East 41st
Denver, Colorado 80216

Great Sand Dunes
    National Monument
11500 Highway 150
Mosca, Colorado 81146

Mesa Verde National Park
(no town name needed)
Colorado 81330

Rabbit Valley Research Natural
    Area and Trail Through Time
362 Main Street
Grand Junction, Colorado 81501

San Juan National Forest
701 Camino Del Rio
Durango, Colorado 81301

New Mexico

Acoma Pueblo Tribal Office
P.O. Box 309
Acoma, New Mexico 87034

Aztec Ruins National Monument
P.O. Box 640
Aztec, New Mexico 87410

Bandelier National Monument
Los Alamos, New Mexico 87544

Carson National Forest
P.O. Box 558
Taos, New Mexico 87571

Chaco Canyon National
    Historical Park
Star Route 4, Box 6500
Bloomfield, New Mexico 87413

Coronado State Monument
P.O. Box 95
Bernalillo, New Mexico 87004

El Malpais National Monument
620 East Santa Fe Street
Grants, New Mexico 87020

El Morro National Monument
Route 2, Box 43
Ramah, New Mexico 87321–9603

New Mexico Department of
    Tourism
1100 S. St. Francis
Santa Fe, New Mexico 87503

Pecos National Monument
P.O. Box 418
Pecos, New Mexico 87552

Petroglyph National Monument
690 Unser NW
Albuquerque, New Mexico 87120

Puye Cliff Dwellings
P.O. Box 580
Espanola, New Mexico 87532

Rio Grande Nature Center
2901 Candelaria NW
Albuquerque, New Mexico 87107

Sandia Ranger District
Cebolla National Forest
11776 Highway 337
Tijeras, New Mexico 87059

Utah

Arches National Park
Box 846
Moab, Utah 84532

Bryce Canyon National Park
Bryce Canyon, Utah 85717

Canyonlands National Park
Moab, Utah 84532

Capitol Reef National Park
Torrey, Utah 84775

Cedar Breaks National Monument
Box 749
Cedar City, Utah 84720

Coral Pink Sand Dunes
State Park
P.O. Box 95
Kanab, Utah 84741

Dinosaur National Monument
Box 210
Dinosaur, Colorado 81610

Dixie Resource Area of the
Bureau of Land Management
225 North Bluff
P.O. Box 726
St. George, Utah 84770

Flaming Gorge National
Recreation Area
P.O. Box 157
Dutch John, Utah 84046

Edge of the Cedars State Park
P.O. Box 788
Blanding, Utah 84511

Escalante Petrified Forest
State Park
P.O. Box 350
Escalante, Utah 84726–0350

Fremont Indian State Park
11000 Clear Creek Canyon Road
Sevier, Utah 84766–9999

Glen Canyon National
Recreation Area
Box 1507
Page, Arizona 86040

Goblin Valley State Park
P.O. Box 93
Green River, Utah 84525–0093

Hovenweep National Monument
McElmo Route
Cortez, Colorado 81321

Kodachrome Basin State Park
P.O. Box 238
Cannonville, Utah 84718

Natural Bridges National
Monument
c/o Canyonlands National Park
Moab, Utah 84532

Pipe Spring National Monument
Moccasin, Arizona 86022

Utah Travel Council
Council Hall/Capitol Hill
Salt Lake City, Utah 84115–1396

Zion National Park
Springdale, Utah 84767–1099

Index

About the Authors

An award-winning writer, Tom Wharton is the outdoor editor at *The Salt Lake City Tribune,* the author of *Utah: A Family Travel Guide,* and co-author with his wife, Gayen, of *Utah* (Compass American Guides). Gayen Wharton is a nationally recognized sixth-grade teacher. The parents of four children, they live in Salt Lake City.

THE MOUNTAINEERS, founded in 1906, is a nonprofit outdoor activity and conservation club, whose mission is "to explore, study, preserve, and enjoy the natural beauty of the outdoors. . . ." Based in Seattle, Washington, the club is now the third-largest such organization in the United States, with 15,000 members and four branches throughout Washington State.

The Mountaineers sponsors both classes and year-round outdoor activities in the Pacific Northwest, which include hiking, mountain climbing, ski-touring, snowshoeing, bicycling, camping, kayaking and canoeing, nature study, sailing, and adventure travel. The club's conservation division supports environmental causes through educational activities, sponsoring legislation, and presenting informational programs. All club activities are led by skilled, experienced volunteers, who are dedicated to promoting safe and responsible enjoyment and preservation of the outdoors.

The Mountaineers Books, an active, nonprofit publishing program of the club, produces guidebooks, instructional texts, historical works, natural history guides, and works on environmental conservation. All books produced by The Mountaineers are aimed at fulfilling the club's mission.

If you would like to participate in these organized outdoor activities or the club's programs, consider a membership in The Mountaineers. For information and an application, write or call The Mountaineers, Club Headquarters, 300 Third Avenue West, Seattle, Washington 98119; (206) 284-6310.

Send or call for our catalog of more than 300 outdoor titles:

The Mountaineers Books
1001 SW Klickitat Way, Suite 201
Seattle, WA 98134
1-800-553-4453